Private AI with Spark

Design, package, and operate private AI locally using Apache Spark, batch pipelines, and vLLM acceleration

Ryein Twardo

Published by: GitforGits

www.gitforgits.com

Printed in India

First Printing: February 2026

ISBN: 978-93-49174-16-0

Cover Design by: Kitten Publishing

Disclaimer:

This book, including all its text, diagrams, and illustrations, is an original work developed for educational and informational purposes. The content is not affiliated with, endorsed by, or sponsored by or any other company, brand, or entity referenced within. All brand names, product names, and trademarks mentioned are the property of their respective owners and are used in a descriptive, educational context only. "Apache," "Apache Spark," "Spark," and the Apache Spark logo are registered trademarks or trademarks of the Apache Software Foundation. All diagrams and illustrations that are not original have been used with proper attribution and credit to their respective sources.

If you believe that any content in this book infringes upon your copyright or trademark, please contact us immediately at support@gitforgits.com. Upon notification, corrective action will be taken promptly.

Prologue

First off, I'm Ryein Twardo, and my whole "AI" thing started out like a lot of tech stories do. I got super pumped, then hit a wall, and then it hit me that the hard part was never the model. The system was a real pain. One time, I remember looking at a dashboard late at night and seeing a pipeline that was working perfectly on my laptop but was having issues in the real world. The networks were spotty, the data was coming in out of order, and the policies were as important as the performance. It's like I had learned how to make predictions. But I hadn't quite figured out how to get predictions to behave right. So, in the middle of the process, from a prototype to a production run, the romance of cleverness kind of fizzled out. And then this new requirement showed up, not invited but still necessary. It was all about being able to do it again. The next day, when someone asked how the output was produced, the answer couldn't be "it worked yesterday." It had to be, "It'll work again, for the same inputs, with the same assets, and we can prove it."

My path to private AI wasn't driven by any particular ideology. I got here because of circumstances I couldn't change. There were security reviews that asked where the data went. They also asked what third parties were involved in processing content. The operations team was wondering what broke when a dependency changed. The leaders wanted results that were reliable without needing someone to stand beside the system and explain what happened. After thinking about it some more, I decided that the best solution was to keep external AI calls to a minimum. Initially, that boundary felt a bit limiting, but then I realized what it provided. All of our datasets, model weights, prompt templates, and run history became ours. It gave us a design that could survive an audit, a network outage, and a change in vendor pricing without collapsing. It also made us more honest because we couldn't hide behind mystery endpoints or unclear "model updates." Every piece of data was stored in our infrastructure, and every output had a clear history. You could say that wasn't a limitation. That was a foundation.

Then Spark came in, and it was like this reliable engine that never asked for extra attention. I had used it before for data processing, but I hadn't treated it as the backbone of private AI. When we stopped going for real-time perfection and started embracing batch discipline, I watched what happened. The data has arrived. We ate it. We've made it into a stable schema. We used defensible cleaning rules. We trained classic models that explained themselves and delivered value fast. We stored the outputs as tables so our system could answer questions, not just generate artifacts. What Spark did was make the work feel steady. It took all the chaotic, raw inputs and turned them into something that was structured and could be queried. So, we could add features without freaking out. You could start by making an extractive summary. We could start with simple labels. Later on, additional acceleration might be added without changing the base architecture. That was the moment I knew this was worth writing down, not as a work of imagination, but as a set of steps that we could follow together and reproduce.

I wrote this book to help the people who come after me, maybe even ourselves in the future, get a leg up. I wanted a path that starts with boundaries, not buzzwords, and ends with a system that runs on schedule, logs what it did, and produces outputs that teams can use. That's why we're building a Private Mailroom Assistant. It's relatable, messy enough to be real, and structured enough to teach. We'll keep our assets under control, our configs explicit, our outputs versioned, and our failures visible. We'll measure instead of assuming. We'll keep the system on track by not making big promises and focusing on small, repeatable steps. If you're holding this book, you're probably tired of prototypes that sparkle once and then disappear. I wrote this because private AI can be practical, and Spark can turn that practicality into a repeatable habit.

Content

Preface

For those who want to build controlled, reproducible AI systems entirely within their own infrastructure, this book is the most practical and implementation-focused trainer. Instead of relying on external APIs or cloud-hosted intelligence services, this book clearly demonstrates how Apache Spark can orchestrate data preparation, model training, batch inference, reporting, and LLM acceleration in a disciplined and transparent way.

As the book opens, it swiftly defines private AI, making it clear that external AI calls are not allowed, full ownership of datasets and model assets is imperative, and repeatable runs with traceable outputs are essential. I will use a realistic sample to show you how to build an end-to-end workflow that ingests raw data, normalizes it into a stable schema, trains a baseline classifier, extracts keywords, generates summaries, and produces structured reports. There's no doubt that each step is implemented with clarity and attention to maintainability. You can be sure that logging, manifests, and monitoring are embedded from the start. We implement classic machine learning techniques, vLLM, performance measurement, batch processing patterns, quarantine handling, and structured metrics to make private AI more usable and compete with cloud-based AI.

Beyond experimentation, the book transitions seamlessly into packaging and routine execution. It will teach you to bundle multiple stages into a single command workflow, schedule daily or weekly runs, generate compact run reports, and adapt the architecture to new datasets without redesigning the system. It does not promise instant transformation or one-click AI solutions. Instead, it provides a structured path to building a sustainable private AI backbone using Spark as the orchestration layer.

In this book you will learn:

- No external AI calls and full control over data, models, and repeatable runs.
- Stable canonical schema with downstream ML and reusable reporting.
- Infuse Classic ML with Spark without introducing LLM complexity.
- Carry out extractive summaries without hallucination risk.
- Complete traceability through manifests, prompt versions, and run logs.
- Implement data and batch flow, along with fast inference using vLLM.
- Extract inspectable data and surface out the hidden errors using quarantine tables.
- Measure and store performance for every run with stakeholder reporting.
- Design single-command pipeline with clear configs to build repeatable AI.

GitforGits

Prerequisites

This book is meant for engineers, data practitioners, and technical leaders who want to understand how to implement controlled AI workflows inside their own environments without depending on external AI services. Prior programming experience with Spark and basics of Generative AI is preferred.

Codes Usage

Are you in need of some helpful code examples to assist you in your programming and documentation? Look no further! Our book offers a wealth of supplemental material, including code examples and exercises.

Not only is this book here to aid you in getting your job done, but you have our permission to use the example code in your programs and documentation. However, please note that if you are reproducing a significant portion of the code, we do require you to contact us for permission.

But don't worry, using several chunks of code from this book in your program or answering a question by citing our book and quoting example code does not require permission. But if you do choose to give credit, an attribution typically includes the title, author, publisher, and ISBN. For example, "Private AI with Spark by Ryein Twardo".

If you are unsure whether your intended use of the code examples falls under fair use or the permissions outlined above, please do not hesitate to reach out to us at support@gitforgits.com.

We are happy to assist and clarify any concerns.

Acknowledgement

I owe a tremendous debt of gratitude to GitforGits, for their unflagging enthusiasm and wise counsel throughout the entire process of writing this book. Their knowledge and careful editing helped make sure the piece was useful for people of all reading levels and comprehension skills. In addition, I'd like to thank everyone involved in the publishing process for their efforts in making this book a reality. Their efforts, from copyediting to advertising, made the project what it is today.

Finally, I'd like to express my gratitude to everyone who has shown me unconditional love and encouragement throughout my life. Their support was crucial to the completion of this book. I appreciate your help with this endeavour and your continued interest in my career.

Hello folks! My core contribution in this book and my responsibility too is to show you to build your own ***private AI platform*** which should be a real, working solution that runs inside your organization's infrastructure, processes sensitive business data, and produces reliable, actionable insights, all without ever sending your information to external servers. No matter if you're just starting out with Spark or you're a pro at designing enterprise data pipelines, I've got you covered. This super-helpful book will walk you through creating a project that's not only practical and easy to understand, but also fits perfectly into private, offline, or regulated settings.

A lot of the time, AI and machine learning feel like they're behind the cloud, public APIs, or big research projects. We're going to break that pattern. This book will show you exactly how to use Apache Spark and carefully selected tools like vLLM to create a reliable, easy-to-audit AI solution. From there, you can handle tasks like classification, keyword extraction, and summarization, starting from raw data and ending with valuable, repeatable results. It's all about being clear and straightforward. We won't make promises we can't keep or use jargon you can't understand. Instead, we'll build skills and habits that make private AI easy to understand and long-lasting.

So, in this book, we will be doing this by developing a sample project, called as ***Mailroom Assistant***. Every technique, file, and workflow you encounter will contribute to this project. The entry-level users will see each piece come together with step-by-step instructions and explanations. And, I am sure the professionals will recognize the best practices in reproducibility, governance, and modular code design. By the end, you will not just know how to use Spark for AI, but also to own your AI.

Preparation

Before we write any code or run our first Spark job, we must lay down the foundation that will keep our project clean, scalable, and resilient as it grows. The best technical books begin by making the reader comfortable and ready for real work. We follow the same tradition in this book.

I must tell you, that a thoughtfully designed project skeleton brings order to what can quickly become a jungle of scripts, logs, and outputs. It allows us to know at a glance where each file lives, what its purpose is, and how it fits into the larger workflow. For beginners, this structure means never getting lost, but for experts, it means every artifact, from models to logs, has a provenance and can be audited.

Our preparation means every asset, output, and log is in its right place—whether we are experimenting on a laptop or running jobs on a production Spark cluster behind several firewalls. We will not be improvising as we go. Instead, we will organize ourselves so that every task—no matter how small—contributes to a predictable, traceable, and repeatable system.

To put it simply, let's picture our workflow as a chain of trusted steps:

- ***Ingest and secure external assets*** (datasets, models, packages), tracking their origin and checksums.
- ***Process and clean data*** in logical, labeled stages (bronze → silver → gold), supporting lineage and easy recovery.

- ***Log every action and result*** for auditing, troubleshooting, and learning.
- ***Separate code from data*** for cleaner development, easier review, and robust productionization.
- ***Version all configuration and prompts*** to support rapid experimentation and governance.

Every new capability, feature, or improvement will fit naturally into this skeleton.

Directory Layout

Once you understand the workflow, we shall begin our project with a top-level folder called **`private-ai-spark/`**. This root will contain only a few, clearly purposed subdirectories and files:

```
private-ai-spark/
  README.md
  pyproject.toml
  configs/
  assets/
  data/
  runs/
  src/
```

From the above directory, the **`configs/`** stores the configuration files and prompt templates. It allows easy updates and full traceability of changes. The **`assets/`** houses all external, immutable resources (datasets, model weights, wheel files) with manifests that record their source and checksums.

The **`data/`** contains all processed outputs, divided into:

- **`bronze/`** for raw, minimally processed ingested data
- **`silver/`** for cleaned and validated datasets, And
- **`gold/`** for enriched outputs, including predictions, summaries, and derived features

`The runs/` includes the logs, metrics, and operational records from every job run. It very well supports the easy troubleshooting and compliance. And, the **`src/`** contains all project source code, organized by logical domains (ingestion, features, machine learning, NLP, LLM).

This is basically the entire project root, from where we make navigation easy for anyone joining the project, and we set ourselves up for scalable, maintainable growth.

Configurations

One of our strongest habits is to put configuration in its own folder, and never get it buried inside code, primarily because it enables us to:

- Switch between development and production settings by simply changing a config file.
- Experiment with new features or models by toggling flags, not rewriting scripts.
- Support auditing by versioning all prompt text and model choices.

For example, a simple **app.yaml** might look like:

```
project:
  name: private-mailroom-assistant
paths:
  assets_root: assets
  data_root: data
  runs_root: runs
dataset:
  enron_sample_root: assets/datasets/enron_sample/raw
features:
  enable_keywords: true
  enable_summarization_baseline: true
  enable_vllm: false
outputs:
  bronze_table: data/bronze/emails_parsed
  silver_table: data/silver/emails_clean
  gold_table: data/gold/emails_enriched
```

Now, with the above feature flags, we can very easily start with only the core features and introduce the advanced capabilities such as vLLM, only when we are ready.

Asset Management

The assets include any external data or code that enters our private environment. They are datasets, model weights, and dependency packages. For every asset, we will:

- Place it in a clearly named folder in assets/
- Attach a manifest.json with its origin, checksum, and any license notes
- Treat it as immutable; every new version gets a new manifest entry

So here, our dataset directory will look something like this:

```
assets/
  datasets/
    enron_sample/
      raw/
      manifest.json
  models/
    llm/
    transformers/
  wheels/
```

This is actually a discipline, and it means that we can always get to know what has entered the system and, if required can recover any required version as needed.

Data Staging

This is very much inspired by the best practices in the data engineering world. I personally alaso agree that the processed data must move through three stages:

- ***Bronze*** which is the raw output from our ingestion jobs. They are parsed, but not cleaned.
- ***Silver*** includes the cleaned, validated, and standardized data. They are ready for feature extraction and modeling. And,
- ***Gold*** which is the enriched data that may include the model predictions, summaries, and some advanced features which are ready for business use or maybe reporting.

If we follow and move our data through these clear stages, we can always reproduce any output from source files and transformations, which also helps us to simplify the debugging and audits.

Logging and Metrics

Every time we run a Spark job, which could be for ingestion, cleaning, feature extraction, or inference, we will be creating a run log and a metrics record in **`runs/`**. These records help us answer key questions, such as:

- Which code and configuration produced this result?
- How long did it take?
- How many records were processed?
- Were there any errors or anomalies?

Having these records as Parquet files means we can use Spark or other tools to query and visualize project health and history. This approach makes our work trustworthy and easy to present to stakeholders.

Code Organization

This is very important one. Inside the **src/**, all our logic is grouped, and that too domain-wise. For example:

- **common/** includes the utilities for paths, logging, and schema definitions
- **ingest/** includes the parsing and raw data loading logic
- **features/** includes the feature engineering scripts, such as TF-IDF extraction
- **ml/** includes the model training and scoring jobs
- **nlp/** contains the keyword extraction and baseline summarization
- **llm/** houses the integration with vLLM for accelerated inference

Each of the domain are isolated, such that the improvements or changes in any of the area do not break the others.

So, before we start messing around with models and more advanced features, we build this project skeleton to set ourselves up with the right habits and workflows. It doesn't matter if you're just starting out or already have experience with private AI. This prep ensures our work will scale, adapt, and stand up to scrutiny. The rest of the project will build on this foundation, chapter by chapter, turning preparation into real results and real results into organizational value.

Chapter 1: Up and Running with Private AI

Overview

In this chapter, you'll learn to set up the groundwork for building your own AI solutions by focusing on practical constraints, clear boundaries, and a repeatable project approach. It will introduce the concept of "private AI" as a workflow where all assets, data, and models are kept entirely within one's own infrastructure, never exposing sensitive information or relying on external APIs. We'll figure out the thinking behind this approach and the perks it brings, like compliance, auditability, and organizational control. We'll help you define the boundaries of your project by creating a clear scope document and adopting a structured, versioned repository layout that supports every step of the process.

We'll figure out what Spark is good at and what it's not so good at. We'll talk about how to use it for stuff it's really good at, like batch processing, big data transformations, and reporting, and how to use other tools for stuff it's not so good at. It'll also explain to keep all your offline assets in order with organized folder layouts and detailed manifest files, so you can always track down any dependency. By the time you're done with this chapter, you'll have the know-how and the skills to make a project skeleton that keeps you from getting overwhelmed and makes sure that future development is doable and realistic.

Concept of "Private AI"

Before we touch any code or talk about data, I want to be honest and precise about what we mean by "private AI." There is a reason to start here, and not with a promise of limitless machine learning. The phrase "private AI" often brings grand images, like limitless automation, conversational agents smarter than any human, or magic analytics that answer any business question on demand. But my or our aim is different. We want to build something real, something reliable, and something that any team with discipline can implement and sustain, without exposing data to the outside world.

In this book, we will not chase the hype or oversell what can be done in a private, air-gapped environment. Instead, we will set out a clear, achievable definition that keeps us honest and our work grounded.

Zero External AI Calls

For us, it's all about keeping things private. Every task, whether it's data prep, training, or inference, runs completely in-house. At no point in the workflow will your data, prompts, or results be sent to an external API or public cloud. This is the most important boundary of our work, and it's the foundation that separates private AI from typical AI deployments that depend on external services.

In my opinion, a true private AI will have following key elements:

- ***No external inference*** means all AI models are running locally. If we use a language model, its weights are stored and loaded from our own disk.

- ***No external data storage*** such that every asset, from the dataset to the model weights to the configuration files, lives inside our perimeter—on our hardware, under our control.

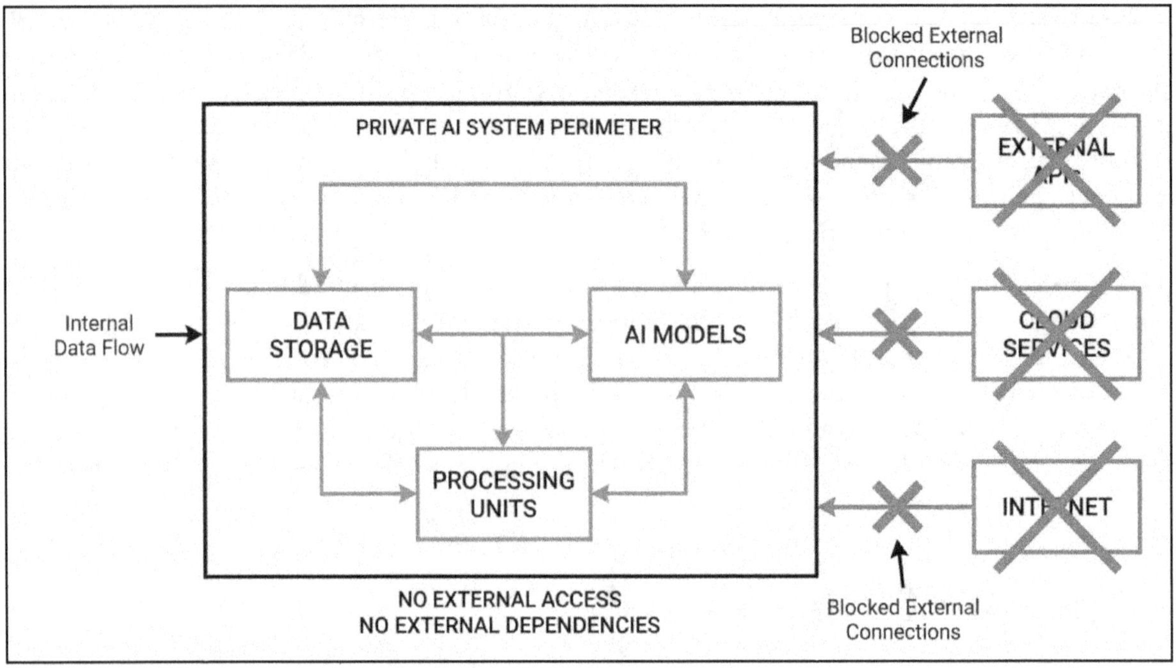

Fig 1.1 'Private-AI' Conceptual View

- ***No cloud services*** as all processing happens within our private cluster or even a single secure server.
- ***No hidden telemetry*** since nothing leaves the system unless we intentionally export it.
- ***No reliance on internet connectivity*** as our system is not only air-gapped by policy; it is operationally independent from any external dependency.

This clear boundary means that sensitive business data—emails, reports, records, whatever the application—never leaves your organization. In practice, this also means we've got to be careful with asset management, model selection, and how we orchestrate batch jobs and logging. We don't have a massive cloud platform to fall back on if something goes wrong; everything needs to be reproducible, repeatable, and auditable right where we run it.

The Power of Private AI

This "zero external AI calls" model does not just protect data. It also brings several advantages and a few trade-offs.

Advantages

- You own the infrastructure, the models, and the outcomes. No vendor can see your data, and you set the policies for access, retention, and deletion.

- Every run, every output, and every artifact is under your governance. If you need to explain or reproduce a result, you have everything you need at hand.
- For industries like healthcare, finance, or government, private AI is often the only path that meets legal and regulatory requirements.
- You decide what models to use, how to train them, and how to structure the pipeline. No vendor-imposed limits.

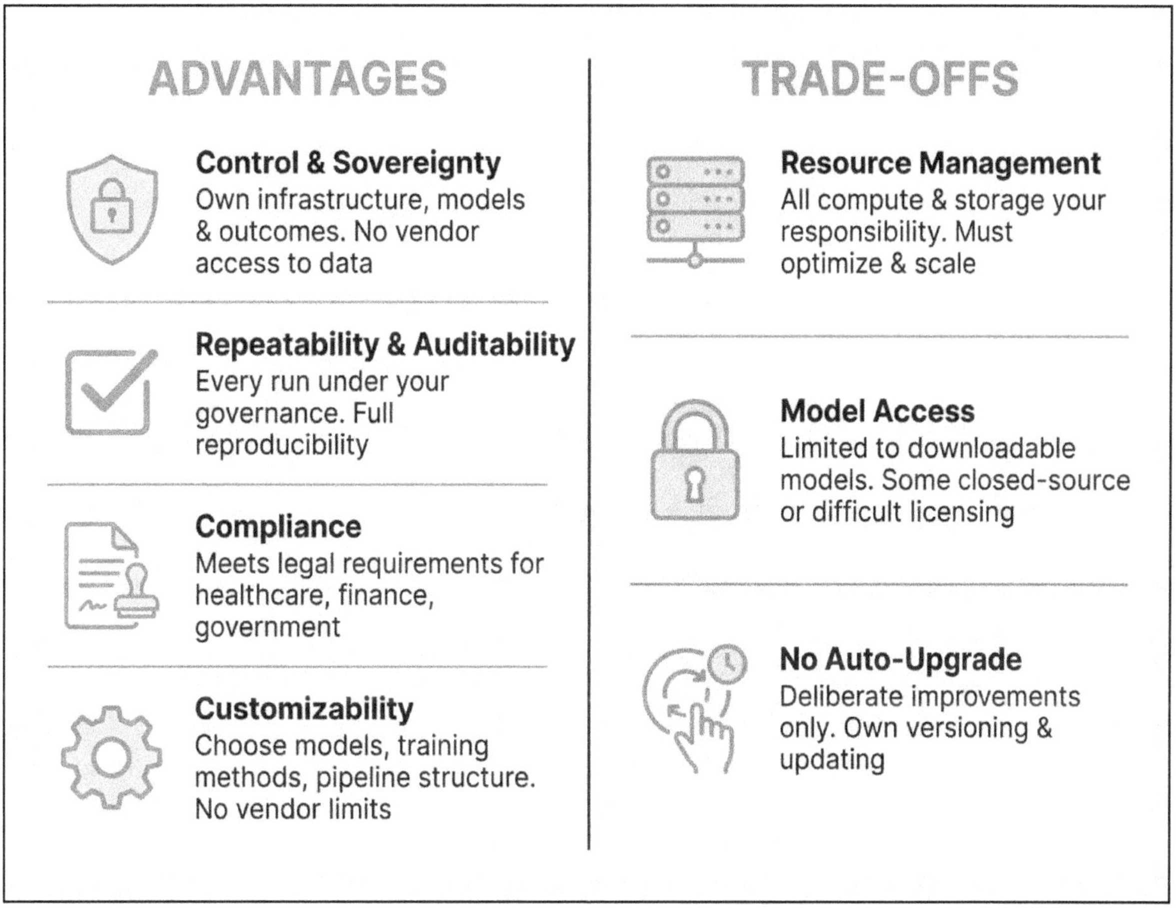

Fig 1.2 Private-AI Benefits vs. Trade-off

Trade-Offs

- All compute and storage are your responsibility. If a model is slow or a dataset is too large, you will need to optimize, scale, or streamline.
- You are limited to what you can download and run offline. Some models are closed-source or require difficult licensing.
- Improvements to code or models must be deliberate, not pushed from outside. You own versioning and updating.

We need to embrace these realities because they force clarity. They can help us scope our work in a way that is both honest and achievable, rather than being lured into building a system that tries to do everything and ends up doing nothing well.

Protected Assets

To make private AI practical, we treat every file as an asset that should be accounted for. This means our data, model weights, configuration files, and even our Python wheels are all stored inside our project repository or secured asset folders.

Nothing is pulled from the internet at runtime. Every dependency is downloaded, checked, and added by us, not a hidden installer or a background sync process. The outcome is a project that can be zipped, shipped, or restored in a new environment with full confidence that it contains all it needs and nothing it should not.

Every new dataset, model, or script enters the system through a clearly defined path:

- ***Assets are fetched and checked***. Whether it is the Enron email dataset, a transformer model, or a supporting Python wheel, we fetch it, verify its checksum, and place it in the **`assets/`** directory.
- ***Nothing is fetched "on demand"***. The Spark jobs never download missing dependencies on the fly. They always fail safely if something is missing, prompting us to resolve it explicitly.
- ***Manifests are kept up to date***. Each asset has an entry in a manifest that records its origin, version, and checksum, ensuring reproducibility.

Repeatable Runs

If a system is not repeatable, it is not trustworthy. Private AI gains much of its power from the discipline of repeatable execution:

- ***Runs can be re-executed with the same results***. The same inputs and configurations will always produce the same outputs.
- We can answer ***"what code, what data, and what model produced this output?"*** for any file in our pipeline.
- ***No random outputs***. Every source of randomness is controlled with a fixed seed.
- Every run records its parameters, performance, and any errors, so we can ***track performance and troubleshoot***.

This repeatability is achieved not with fancy workflow engines, but with careful design of our file structure, configuration, and logging. We ensure every job has a clear input, a defined output, and a visible trail of what happened.

Project Repo Review

It's time to go over the project structure we talked about before. This isn't just a routine part of our process; it's our commitment to keep things organized, easy to understand, and safe from the very start.

```
private-ai-spark/
  README.md
  pyproject.toml
  configs/
    app.yaml
    spark.yaml
    prompts/
      summarize_v1.txt
  assets/
    datasets/
      enron_sample/
        raw/
        manifest.json
    models/
      llm/
      transformers/
    wheels/
  data/
    bronze/
    silver/
    gold/
  runs/
    logs/
    metrics/
  src/
    mailroom/
      __init__.py
```

```
    cli.py
    common/
      __init__.py
      paths.py
      logging.py
      schema.py
    ingest/
      __init__.py
      parse_email.py
      ingest_job.py
    features/
      __init__.py
      tfidf_job.py
    ml/
      __init__.py
      train_job.py
      score_job.py
    nlp/
      __init__.py
      keywords_job.py
      summarize_baseline.py
    llm/
      __init__.py
      vllm_client.py
      vllm_batch_job.py
```

Each of the directories has a purpose, like the:

- **`assets/`** stores every immutable input from the outside world.
- **`data/`** stores our intermediate and final results, moving through bronze, silver, and gold stages for clarity.
- **`runs/`** contains logs and metrics for every job.

- **src/** holds our code, strictly separated from data and assets.
- **configs/** keeps all our settings, making every run reproducible and auditable.

Short Scope Project Document

In professional practice and to the best of my experience, teams prefer to begin every critical project with a written scope. We will do the same. This scope document does not need to be long, but it should be explicit about what we are building and what we are not building.

For this, we will create a file in your project as **private-ai-spark/SCOPE.md**.

And, the below thing is what our scope document will say:

```
# SCOPE.md

## Private Mailroom Assistant — Project Scope

### **Objective**
Develop a private, in-house AI-powered assistant for
processing and analyzing internal mail archives. The system
will ingest emails, classify messages, extract keywords, and
generate concise summaries — all within a fully private
environment. No data, prompts, or results will be sent to any
external service or cloud API.

### **What Will Be Built**
- **Deterministic ingestion pipeline:**
  Parses raw email files into structured tables suitable for
analysis.
- **Staged data processing flow:**
  Data passes through bronze (raw parsed), silver (cleaned and
standardized), and gold (enriched with
predictions/tags/summaries) stages for clarity and
reproducibility.
- **Feature extraction routines:**
  Produces representations for ML tasks, such as TF-IDF
vectors and other engineered features.
- **Baseline machine learning model:**
  Trains a transparent classifier (e.g., logistic regression
or decision tree) for categorizing emails.
- **Batch inference and reporting jobs:**
  Processes new emails in batches, outputs classifications and
keyword tags, and produces human-readable reports.
- **Extractive summarization:**
```

Generates concise summaries of emails using rules or classical NLP techniques.
- **Optional LLM-powered summarization (offline):**
  Accelerates and improves summaries using a locally hosted vLLM server and offline models (such as DistilBERT, Llama 2, or Falcon-7B) when hardware and licenses permit.
- **Configuration, logging, and run-tracking:**
  Ensures every job and result is reproducible and auditable.
- **Asset management:**
  All datasets, models, and dependencies are tracked with manifests and checksums.
- **Comprehensive documentation:**
  Documents every major job, artifact, input, output, and configuration file for future maintainers.

**What Will Not Be Built**
- **No live chatbots or interactive real-time web apps**
  This is a batch-first, offline system.
- **No external API calls for inference, data storage, or analytics**
  All processing is strictly on-premises, inside the organization's infrastructure.
- **No closed, proprietary models requiring cloud connections or license violations**
  Only open, auditable models that can be hosted privately are included.
- **No advanced neural architecture research or leaderboard chasing**
  Focus remains on reliability, transparency, and repeatability, not bleeding-edge accuracy.
- **No black-box AutoML or invisible automation**
  Every workflow step will be explicit and reviewable.
- **No multi-user or advanced access control frameworks**
  The system is designed for a single team or project; organizational-level user management is out of scope.

**Intended Audience**
- Data engineers and developers who need to process sensitive data in regulated or private environments.
- Professionals in sectors such as finance, healthcare, government, or critical infrastructure, where data must never leave internal networks.

```
- Anyone interested in building a reliable, maintainable, and
auditable private AI workflow using Apache Spark and
supporting tools.

### **Project Boundaries**
- **Everything is air-gapped or offline:**
  No workflow step will require internet access after the
initial setup of assets and dependencies.
- **All artifacts are versioned and auditable:**
  Datasets, models, and configurations are tracked, and every
output can be traced to its inputs and code version.
- **Focus is on clarity, not complexity:**
  The project will always prefer solutions that are
explainable and maintainable, avoiding unnecessary abstraction
or technical debt.
_This document is to be reviewed and updated before every
major release or when a significant change to project goals or
boundaries is proposed.
```

Once you are done with documenting the above scope, we will just place this **SCOPE.md** in our project root.

Setting Realistic Expectations

With the above boundaries and scope, our expectations are clear. We are not promising to deliver the world's most accurate AI, or an interface that can answer any question in milliseconds. Instead, we are guaranteeing a robust, defensible, and repeatable system that any organization can operate with confidence.

- If you follow along, you will be able to reproduce every result, audit every decision, and adapt the project for your own data and policies.
- You will be able to tell immediately what the system does, what it cannot do, and why.
- By the end, you will have all the skills and artifacts needed to build private AI solutions for real business needs, without hidden risks or surprises.

This is private AI, ***without hype***. With these boundaries in place, we are ready to move forward, confident in what we will achieve—and just as importantly, confident in what we will intentionally leave out. Our next topic will move from concept to concrete, beginning the real work of building the Mailroom Assistant, step by step, within our clearly defined scope.

Spark Contribution to Private AI

To build a reliable and sustainable private AI system, we must match every tool to its natural strengths and recognize its boundaries. Too many projects struggle because they expect a tool to solve problems it was never designed for. The Spark is a very powerful engine, but it is not a magic wand. Our project will be successful only if we lean on Spark for the tasks it does exceptionally well, and avoid forcing it into roles where it is inefficient or unsuited.

This topic will help us build honest, achievable expectations and a system design that lasts. We will map the major tasks of private AI into two clear buckets:

1. **Tasks Spark excels at**
2. **Tasks Spark should never be asked to perform**

Apache Spark is a distributed compute engine, designed to scale across dozens or hundreds of machines, or to deliver robust throughput on a single server. In private AI, the Spark becomes our backbone for high-volume, repeatable batch work. Its strengths are well-proven and align perfectly with many real business needs.

Spark's Sweet Spots

Batch Data Preparation

Spark's DataFrame API, inspired by the best of SQL and pandas, is built for processing large, tabular datasets. When we ingest data (for example, parsing hundreds of thousands of emails), the Spark helps us:

- Read from many files or data sources in parallel
- Clean, normalize, and transform columns using expressive code
- Apply validation, deduplication, and enrichment in bulk
- Materialize outputs efficiently (in Parquet, ORC, or CSV) for future steps

Every time we transform data from "raw" to "clean," or join different sources, the Spark gives us a performance and reproducibility advantage. No single-node script or desktop spreadsheet can keep up with Spark's speed or reliability in this role.

Batch Feature Engineering and Transformation

Before any machine learning, we need to extract and transform features. The Spark is ideal for:

- Generating TF-IDF matrices, word embeddings, or numerical features for millions of rows
- Applying user-defined functions (UDFs) at scale
- Assembling, normalizing, or scaling features for input to a model
- Persisting feature tables for audit and reuse

These steps can run overnight or on a schedule—Spark thrives when the job is "take a big chunk of data, apply complex logic, and produce a structured output."

Batch Model Training and Scoring

Spark's MLlib is designed to fit classical models (logistic regression, decision trees, clustering) on massive datasets. Even when we want to use more modern models (like ONNX-converted transformers or simple neural networks), the Spark remains the right platform for:

- Training on big data, using distributed algorithms
- Running batch inference: scoring millions of rows, emails, or records at once
- Partitioning workloads for efficient parallelism
- Capturing model outputs as DataFrames for further analysis

Every time we need to score a large backlog, re-train a model from scratch, or process a new data dump, the Spark's batch orientation is a clear advantage.

Audit Logging, Lineage, and Compliance at Scale

When our environment demands strong governance, the Spark helps by:

- Generating logs for every run
- Recording input and output sizes, errors, and timing
- Supporting lineage tracking with Spark event logs or custom metadata

Because Spark can write logs and metrics as tables, it makes downstream audit and reporting practical and scalable.

Large-Scale Joins, Aggregations, and Analytics

If our workflow requires us to join, aggregate, or summarize data—such as producing daily reports, time-series trends, or operational dashboards—Spark's distributed SQL engine is efficient and reliable.

For all its power, the Spark is not a fit for every AI or data task. If we push it beyond its natural domain, we encounter pain points: slowdowns, complexity, and brittle systems that are hard to debug. In private AI, the cost of misuse is even higher—since every run consumes our own resources and is not rescued by elastic cloud magic.

Spark's Failure Zone

Low-Latency, Real-Time, and Interactive Serving

Spark was designed for batch. While newer versions add structured streaming and micro-batch processing, the Spark is fundamentally not a real-time engine.

- If the goal is to serve a chatbot with sub-second responses, the Spark will always lag behind specialized services.
- When the system needs to process streaming data with millisecond latency (such as IoT telemetry, live webhooks, or interactive applications), tools like Flink, Kafka Streams, or dedicated application servers are better choices.
- We must never design for chat serving, web interfaces, or conversational agents to be

powered by Spark directly.

Stateful, Long-Lived Microservices

Spark jobs are transient—they start, run, finish, and shut down. Long-lived services that must keep in-memory state (like an always-on recommendation API or user session manager) are outside Spark's wheelhouse.

Advanced Deep Learning Model Training

While Spark integrates with deep learning frameworks (through project integrations like BigDL, TensorFlowOnSpark, or Horovod), its strength is not in GPU-accelerated, research-heavy training loops. If we want to train massive transformer models from scratch, or require tight feedback cycles for model experimentation, frameworks like PyTorch or TensorFlow (run on dedicated GPU nodes) are more appropriate.

Spark can manage data movement and orchestration, but the core model training step is better left to other engines.

GPU-Intensive LLM Serving

For the step where we run large language models (LLMs) at high throughput, vLLM or similar inference servers are a much better fit. The Spark can orchestrate calls to these services in batch, but Spark itself should not be expected to execute LLM inference directly—especially when GPU scheduling, memory management, and high concurrency are required.

Interactive User Interfaces and Direct User Requests

Spark's startup time, batch orientation, and job scheduling make it unsuitable as the backend for dashboards, ad-hoc queries, or any "click-and-wait" system. For interactive needs, pair Spark with tools designed for rapid feedback, such as lightweight API servers, dashboards (e.g., Streamlit), or direct database queries.

Mapping Project Tasks

Let us see how our own Mailroom Assistant project looks when we apply these buckets. The bucket one will be the tasks Spark does well:

- Parsing and structuring large volumes of emails (ingest jobs)
- Cleaning, validating, and standardizing text data (cleaning jobs)
- Generating features like TF-IDF, basic NLP enrichment, or summary statistics
- Training and applying classical ML models for classification and tagging
- Orchestrating batch calls to vLLM or other LLM inference engines
- Writing and aggregating audit logs and metrics for every batch run
- Producing batch reports and analytics outputs for further review

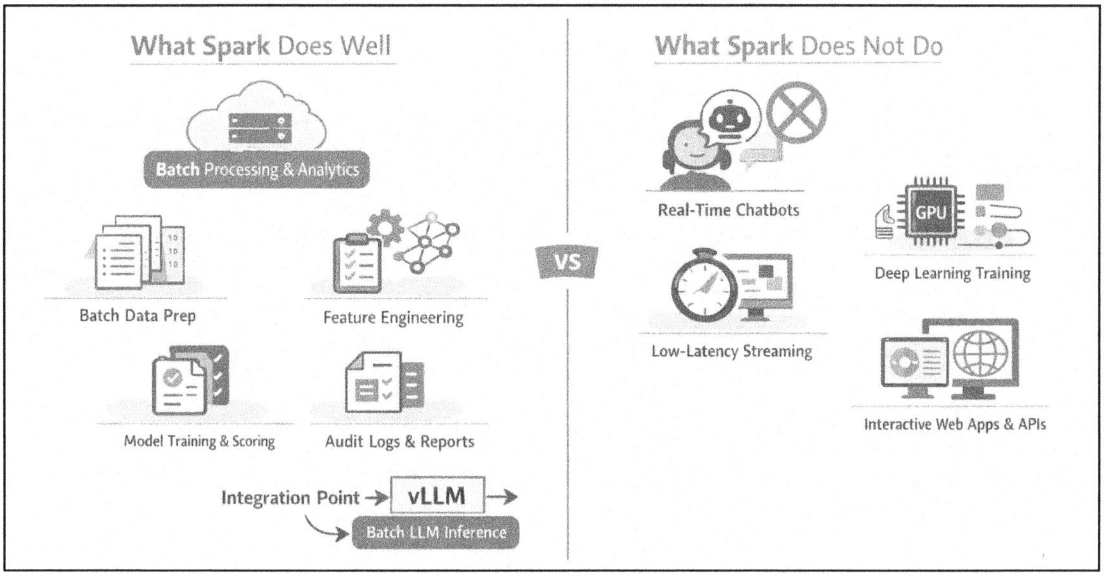

Fig 1.3 Spark's Capability Mapping

And the bucket two lists the tasks Spark should not handle:

- Powering interactive chatbots, real-time user queries, or web UIs
- Serving online APIs for external access or direct user interaction
- Training massive deep learning models with intensive GPU requirements (beyond what batch jobs can handle)
- Running GPU-bound inference loops natively (leave to vLLM or equivalent)
- Maintaining long-lived, stateful services

Single-Page Architecture Brief

Based out on mapping the tasks, we will now make a note of it into a one-page not saved in **`private-ai-spark/docs/ARCHITECTURE.md`** shown as below:

```
# ARCHITECTURE.md
## System Task Map
### Tasks Owned by Spark
- Batch ingestion of emails and assets
- Data cleaning, validation, and transformation
- Feature engineering and batch statistics
- ML training and batch inference with classical models
- Batch orchestration of external summarization (vLLM)
```

```
- Metrics, logs, and lineage reporting
### Tasks Delegated to Other Tools
- Interactive chatbots or web applications (not implemented)
- Real-time, low-latency data pipelines (not implemented)
- Deep learning model training on GPU clusters (not implemented)
- High-concurrency LLM inference (owned by vLLM)
- User-facing API endpoints or dashboards (not implemented)
### Integration Points
- Spark writes input for vLLM summarization jobs, collects outputs in the next batch step.
- All services communicate via file handoff or batch APIs, never real-time calls.
```

This mapping will be placed in our repository to set expectations and prevent accidental scope creep. If someone asks, "Can we add a real-time chatbot?" and our answer should be ready, which is ***not with Spark***. If someone wants to know if we can scale batch analytics or add new data sources, then ***Spark is*** our clear answer.

After drawing a clear line between what Spark should and should not do, we build a private AI system that will last. Our work becomes predictable, manageable, and aligned with Spark's true capabilities.

In our next topic, we will define our sample project "***Mailroom Assistant***" in more detail, so we always know exactly what we are building, and why Spark is the right foundation for each step.

Project 'Private Mailroom Assistant'

Our journey through private AI centers on a single, evolving project i.e. the ***Private Mailroom Assistant***. We make sure that every new idea, skill, or line of code contributes to a coherent, meaningful system by anchoring every chapter and hands-on lesson to this project. That way, you won't get overloaded with information, and even the most advanced topics will be clearly connected to real business value.

The private mailroom assistant is designed to operate entirely within your organization's secure environment. Its job is to take raw, unstructured internal emails and convert them into structured, tagged, summarized, and reportable knowledge—without ever sending a byte outside your infrastructure. All the steps, from the simplest batch job to the most advanced language model inference, will be put into this single project thread, audited, and evolved.

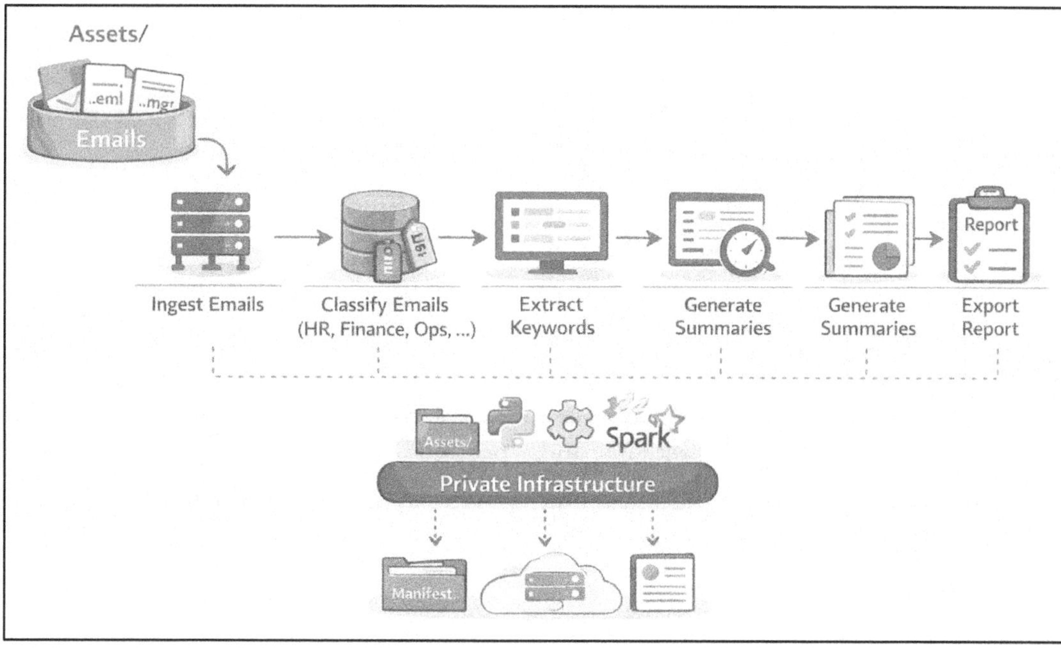

Fig 1.4 Project Overview

In the following, we will define and explore each of the five core features that make our private mailroom assistant practical, valuable, and achievable:

Ingesting Emails

The raw emails are messy. And, parsing them into a reliable schema is the foundation for every downstream task. Without this, tasks like classification, keyword extraction, and summarization become unreliable or impossible.

So here, we will load a large set of email files from our internal storage, parse their metadata and content, and structure them into a Spark DataFrame. The supported formats might include **`.eml`**, **`.mbox`**, or similar, and every email will yield fields such as sender, recipients, sent time, subject, and body.

Let me brief you with a quick overview on the practical steps:

- We at first create an **`ingest_job.py`** script under **`src/mailroom/ingest/`**.
- We then use the Spark's DataFrame API to batch process files in **`assets/datasets/enron_sample/raw/`**.
- After this, we will then parse and store the output as a Parquet table in **`data/bronze/emails_parsed`**.

```
# src/mailroom/ingest/ingest_job.py
from pyspark.sql import SparkSession
```

```
def run_ingest(input_dir, output_path):
    spark =
SparkSession.builder.appName("MailroomIngest").getOrCreate()
    # [Add parsing logic here]
    # df.write.mode("overwrite").parquet(output_path)
    # print(f"Ingested N emails into {output_path}")
```

Classifying Emails into Tags

The tags primarily help to organize overwhelming volumes of email into actionable groups, allowing focused review, compliance audits, and reporting.

So here in our project, after ingestion, we will use a classical ML model, like logistic regression to assign each email to one or more categories such as HR, Finance, Operations, Legal, or Personal.

And to do it, we will:

- First place the labeled examples in a CSV sidecar.
- We then implement training in **src/mailroom/ml/train_job.py**.
- Next, we then score all emails in batch using **src/mailroom/ml/score_job.py**.
- And, finally we store the classified results in **data/gold/emails_tagged**.

```
# src/mailroom/ml/train_job.py
# [Train classifier using Spark MLlib]
# src/mailroom/ml/score_job.py
# [Score incoming emails, append 'tags' column]
```

Extracting Keywords

The keywords, in general, primarily power the search, filtering, and fast content discovery. Even the simple keyword extraction provides immediate business value.

So here, in our project, each email will be analyzed to extract a concise set of keywords that represent its core topics or entities, using TF-IDF or other NLP methods. Following is a way, this will be done:

- We will make use of the Spark MLlib's TF-IDF transformer in **src/mailroom/features/keywords_job.py**.
- Next, for each email, we will then compute the ***top-scoring*** terms and attach as a **keywords** column in the DataFrame.
- Finally, we will then store output in **data/gold/emails_keywords**.

```
# src/mailroom/features/keywords_job.py
# [TF-IDF computation and keyword extraction]
```

Generating Short Summaries

The summaries are meant to save time for end-users, condense critical communications, and help surface important information buried in long threads.

In our project, referring to the selected emails (e.g., those with long bodies, or sent to many recipients), we will generate a concise summary—starting with rule-based extraction, then optionally upgrading to LLM-powered summarization using vLLM.

Following is a quick way to do it:

- We will first get the baseline extraction summarizer implemented in the **src/mailroom/nlp/summarize_baseline.py**.
- After this, the summaries are stored in **data/gold/emails_summarized** as a **summary** column.

```
# src/mailroom/nlp/summarize_baseline.py
# [Simple extractive summarizer logic]
```

Exporting Batch Report

The reporting closes the loop, providing auditable, actionable outputs for stakeholders. It ensures every run is measurable and improvements are visible over time. In our project, the system will produce a batch report summarizing the run: counts of ingested, tagged, summarized emails, tag distributions, top keywords, and any errors or anomalies.

For this,

- We will write a reporting script in **src/mailroom/common/report_job.py**.
- And then, we will aggregate statistics and output as CSV or Markdown in **runs/**.

```
# src/mailroom/common/report_job.py
# [Aggregate and export processing stats]
```

Maintaining Single Project Thread

Since we're not starting from scratch with each technique, we just weave every lesson, script, and output into the Mailroom Assistant as it's evolving. This single-threaded approach makes progress visible, reduces rework, and keeps every improvement relevant to a shared goal. Each step builds on the last, so you always see how theory turns into practice—and how small wins add up to a valuable system.

Every new skill adds to:

- The same codebase
- The same configuration patterns
- The same logging and reporting habits
- The same assets and data directories

First Real Implementation

This is a small implementation of our project, and something you can mimic right away. Let us say that we have a small batch of emails in **assets/datasets/enron_sample/raw/**:

As we learned, we will first run the ingestion job:

```
python src/mailroom/ingest/ingest_job.py
```

We then run the classifier training job (with our labeled sample):

```
python src/mailroom/ml/train_job.py
```

Next is to score all emails for tags:

```
python src/mailroom/ml/score_job.py
```

After this, we will then extract the keywords:

```
python src/mailroom/features/keywords_job.py
```

Once the keywords are extracted, it is easy to generate the summaries for selected emails:

```
python src/mailroom/nlp/summarize_baseline.py
```

And finally, we will export the report:

```
python src/mailroom/common/report_job.py
```

While executing each of the above steps, I recommend that you keep checking the **data/** and **runs/** directories for outputs, logs, and metrics. This will mentor us to adjust the configurations as needed to control which features are enabled and how results are formatted.

All I can say is that, every time you write a script, configure a run, or inspect an output, you are building private AI in a way that is repeatable, auditable, and genuinely useful—all while reducing cognitive load and maximizing real-world skills. This is the heart of our approach and the guarantee that no lesson will be wasted or left unconnected.

Offline Assets Folder

In private AI development, the way we organize and track our datasets, model checkpoints, and package files makes the difference between a system that is secure and sustainable—and one that is unmanageable or risky. We are not simply collecting files; we are establishing a culture of discipline, traceability, and confidence.

For our Mailroom Assistant project, we commit to a structure that is logical to humans and straightforward for scripts to manage. It guarantees us that no dependency or data source ever appears as a "mystery file." Instead, everything has a home and a story.

Building Folder Structure

To keep our offline assets predictable, we will create three main subdirectories under **`assets/`**: one each for datasets, models, and Python wheels (package files). Each category will have a further organized layout.

We can visualize the top-level folder structure like this:

```
private-ai-spark/
  assets/
    datasets/
    models/
    wheels/
```

Let us walk through how we might set up these directories for a real, growing project.

- Each dataset receives its own folder under **`datasets/`**, such as **`enron_sample/`**. Inside, we keep the raw files and a record of their source and checksums.
- Each language model—whether Llama 2, DistilBERT, or something else—gets a dedicated folder under **`models/`**, including any subfolders for weights and a manifest that details its provenance.
- All external Python package files that we intend to use for local, offline installation go in the **`wheels/`** directory. This is where we store Spark, vLLM, Spark NLP, or any other wheels not available on our environment by default.

The layout becomes, for example:

```
assets/
```

```
datasets/
  enron_sample/
    raw/
    manifest.json
models/
  llm/
    llama2/
      weights/
      manifest.json
    distilbert/
      weights/
      manifest.json
wheels/
  pyspark-3.5.0-py3-none-any.whl
  spark_nlp-5.2.0-py3-none-any.whl
  vllm-0.4.0-py3-none-any.whl
  manifest.json
```

With this structure, every asset is stored offline, versioned by folder and documented by manifest.

Crafting Manifest

A well-managed offline asset is never anonymous. For every dataset, model, or package file, we maintain a manifest, typically as **manifest.json** alongside the artifact itself. This manifest serves as a ledger, providing not just a list of files but a history of where they came from, what they are, their integrity hash, their version, any licensing or usage notes, and the date they joined our project.

For instance, after downloading the Enron Email Dataset and verifying it, we enter its details into the manifest like this:

```
{
  "artifacts": [
    {
      "name": "enron_sample_raw.tar.gz",
```

```
      "type": "dataset",
      "source_url":
"https://www.cs.cmu.edu/~enron/enron_mail_20150507.tar.gz",
      "sha256":
"ed8d123e429a488e0be24cbd1d32b2a8e6f2cf23b7e57da7f4e6349e3ef56
78a",
      "version": "2015-05-07",
      "license": "Research only; see dataset site",
      "date_added": "2024-02-12"
    }
  ]
}
```

In the case of adding a model, such as Llama 2, the manifest in **models/llm/llama2/manifest.json** would record the following:

```
{
  "artifacts": [
    {
      "name": "llama-2-7b-chat.Q4_K_M.gguf",
      "type": "model",
      "source_url": "https://huggingface.co/TheBloke/Llama-2-
7B-GGUF/resolve/main/llama-2-7b-chat.Q4_K_M.gguf",
      "sha256":
"3a1b10aa7e119cb19c1bfcfafdcfb4e2e09e9ed2b5020c624d807fb2d84a0
b07",
      "version": "7B Q4_K_M",
      "license": "Meta LLAMA 2 License",
      "date_added": "2024-02-12"
    }
  ]
}
```

For our package files, a similar manifest at **`assets/wheels/manifest.json`** ensures we can always answer, "Where did this wheel come from? Which version did we use? What license applies?"

```
{
  "artifacts": [
    {
      "name": "pyspark-3.5.0-py3-none-any.whl",
      "type": "wheel",
      "source_url":
"https://pypi.org/project/pyspark/3.5.0/#files",
      "sha256":
"07f86e3dfb2196e31366ac7fef8d3245b65522ae5a3f60b5c2e7ad37e481f
f10",
      "version": "3.5.0",
      "license": "Apache-2.0",
      "date_added": "2024-02-12"
    },
    {
      "name": "vllm-0.4.0-py3-none-any.whl",
      "type": "wheel",
      "source_url":
"https://pypi.org/project/vllm/0.4.0/#files",
      "sha256":
"c2c0f07d91899f04eae6b6682451ef9de8031c4b8e5134a8fa1ce308c4025
f23",
      "version": "0.4.0",
      "license": "Apache-2.0",
      "date_added": "2024-02-12"
    }
  ]
}
```

Calculating and Recording Checksums

Every time we add a new file—whether it is a dataset archive, a model checkpoint, or a Python wheel—we must record its SHA-256 checksum. This acts as the digital fingerprint of the artifact.

To compute this on most systems, we can use:

```
sha256sum filename.whl
```

Or, if we want to make use of Python, then the following:

```
import hashlib
def sha256sum(filename):
    h = hashlib.sha256()
    with open(filename, "rb") as f:
        for chunk in iter(lambda: f.read(4096), b""):
            h.update(chunk)
    return h.hexdigest()
```

We add these values to your manifest. This ensures that anyone can verify that the asset has not been corrupted or replaced.

Adding New Asset

To start with, we will first ***Download*** the new dataset, model, or wheel to your local machine.

After this, we then ***Compute its SHA-256 hash*** using the methods taught in the previous topic.

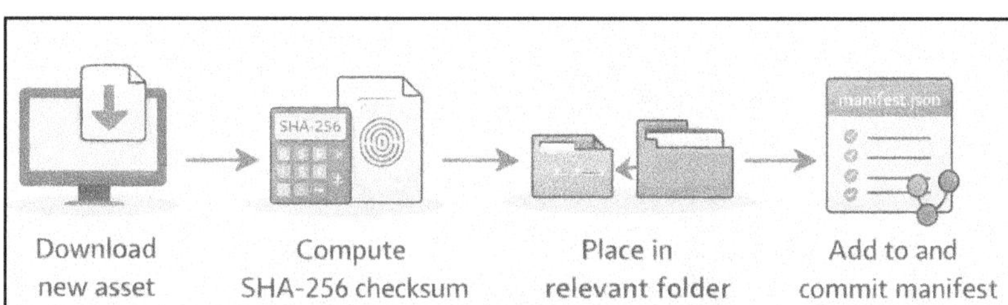

Fig 1.5 Project Asset Addition

Next, we then ***place the file*** in the correct subdirectory under **`assets/`** (datasets, models, or wheels). After this, we then ***edit/create the manifest*** in that directory, including adding an entry for the new artifact with all relevant details like name, type, source URL, checksum, version, license, and date added.

And finally, we will then ***commit both the file and manifest*** to version control. This ensures history is preserved and every asset update is visible and auditable.

Such above structure and discipline treat our datasets, models, and wheels as first-class citizens. The offline assets folder becomes a stepping stone for everything we build. Every new team member, reviewer, or compliance officer will know immediately: this project takes asset management seriously, and every result is built on firm ground.

Summary

In this chapter, we established a clear and pragmatic foundation for building private AI by defining exactly what "private AI" means in our setup and setting realistic boundaries. We explained that all AI tasks would be executed within the organization's own infrastructure, with no data, models, or logs ever sent outside the controlled environment. We described a disciplined project repository layout and crafted a dedicated scope document to ensure the work remained achievable, auditable, and tailored for repeatability. We mapped every task into two distinct buckets, matching Spark's strengths to large-scale, batch-oriented processing while avoiding the temptation to use it for real-time or interactive services. Our step-by-step process emphasized a single project thread with cumulative learning, from ingesting and classifying emails to keyword extraction, summarization, and reporting.

Along the way, we gave special attention to the management of offline assets, creating predictable folder layouts for datasets, models, and wheels, and maintaining manifest files with source URLs and checksums for full traceability. We demonstrated how each asset's lineage could be verified, supporting compliance and reproducibility. As a result, we ended the chapter with a robust, transparent, and manageable private AI project skeleton—setting the stage for all future development to remain honest, auditable, and realistic.

CHAPTER 2: DATA WORKFLOWS USING SPARK DATAFRAMES

Overview

We now land up in chapter 2. And, here in this chapter, we will learn to make data as the centerpiece of our private AI project. We start with introducing the Enron Email Dataset and learn to select a safe, manageable subset rather than working with overwhelming data volumes from the start. We will learn to organize raw email files alongside their cleaned, normalized outputs, ensuring that every step is transparent and repeatable. Together, we will design a clear schema for emails and implement a robust parser to extract the most important fields into a Spark DataFrame, which is very useful for every future feature.

Later, we will learn to apply minimal and defendable cleaning rules that are easy to explain and justify. We will put in place lightweight data quality checks that run every time—asserting schema correctness, checking for nulls, and monitoring basic distributions—so that problems are caught early and documented clearly. You will learn to implement audit-friendly logging, capturing the dataset version, code state, and output paths for every run in a simple, queryable format. By the end of this chapter, you will be equipped with all the practical skills and discipline required to build trustworthy, auditable, and maintainable data workflows for advanced analytics and private AI applications.

Dataset Choice

When we start a private AI project, it is tempting to grab a massive dataset and jump right into coding. However, experience has shown us that the most confident progress comes from starting small. We pick a sample we can see, touch, and debug easily, letting us spot mistakes early and adapt quickly. We can think of it as building with blocks, not pouring concrete all at once. We will keep our focus on baby steps, making sure every step is solid before we go bigger.

Enron Email Dataset Overview

For our first experiments, we are turning to the Enron Email Dataset—a treasure trove of real emails exchanged by Enron employees. It is a classic in the data science world, and you will find it referenced in everything from academic NLP research to practical email filtering projects.

We can download the full dataset directly from Carnegie Mellon University or you may simply click the download link: https://www.cs.cmu.edu/~enron/enron_mail_20150507.tar.gz. It is big, over 500,000 emails, so we are not going to tackle all of it at once. After extracting the archive, we will handpick just a few user folders or .eml files, aiming for something in the ballpark of 100 to 500 emails. This will keep our Spark jobs quick and our logs readable.

Once we have our subset, we will then keep it in its own special corner of our project:

```
private-ai-spark/assets/datasets/enron_sample/raw/
```

That way, our raw data is always safe and easy to find, and we avoid accidental mix-ups down the line.

Setting up Storage

While working with real data, it means we want to always know exactly where it came from and how it changes along the way. So here, we keep both the raw files and the processed output side-by-side.

So here, we will set up our project folders like this:

- The raw emails go into **assets/datasets/enron_sample/raw/**.
- As soon as we parse and clean them, we drop the output into **data/bronze/emails_parsed/**.

The Parquet will be our format of choice for the processed data since it is lightning-fast with Spark and super easy to query. Our pipeline can easily read from raw, write to Parquet, and never overwrite the originals.

Building Ingestion Script

We will now begin with writing a little Spark job. And it is to bring the emails into our system. So here, we will start simple like, we will open each .eml file, pull out a few fields, and store them as rows in a DataFrame.

Following is how we will set it up:

```
# src/mailroom/ingest/ingest_job.py
from pyspark.sql import SparkSession
from pyspark.sql.types import StructType, StructField,
StringType, TimestampType
import os
def parse_email(file_path):
    # We will plug in a real parser later; for now, we keep it
simple
    return {
        "file_path": file_path,
        "sender": "unknown",
        "recipients": "unknown",
        "sent_at": None,
```

```
        "subject": "placeholder subject",
        "body": "placeholder body"
    }
def run_ingest(input_dir, output_path):
    spark =
SparkSession.builder.appName("MailroomIngest").getOrCreate()
    schema = StructType([
        StructField("file_path", StringType(), True),
        StructField("sender", StringType(), True),
        StructField("recipients", StringType(), True),
        StructField("sent_at", TimestampType(), True),
        StructField("subject", StringType(), True),
        StructField("body", StringType(), True),
    ])
    files = [os.path.join(input_dir, f) for f in
os.listdir(input_dir) if f.endswith(".eml")]
    records = [parse_email(fp) for fp in files]
    df = spark.createDataFrame(records, schema)
    df.write.mode("overwrite").parquet(output_path)
    print(f"Ingested {len(records)} emails into
{output_path}")
if __name__ == "__main__":
    run_ingest("assets/datasets/enron_sample/raw",
"data/bronze/emails_parsed")
```

After this, we will have a handful of .eml files ready. Next, we now run the script:

```
python src/mailroom/ingest/ingest_job.py
```

This will create our very first normalized Parquet output, which is just right next to the raw data.

Creating Manifest

No one likes mystery files. In our project, as we set up our dataset, we will jot down its origin, version, and checksum in a manifest. This little JSON file lives in **assets/datasets/enron_sample/manifest.json** and acts as our "passport" for the data.

Following is how our manifest will look like:

```
{
  "artifacts": [
    {
      "name": "enron_sample_raw.tar.gz",
      "type": "dataset",
      "source_url":
"https://www.cs.cmu.edu/~enron/enron_mail_20150507.tar.gz",
      "sha256":
"ed8d123e429a488e0be24cbd1d32b2a8e6f2cf23b7e57da7f4e6349e3ef56
78a",
      "version": "2015-05-07",
      "license": "Research only; see dataset site",
      "date_added": "2024-02-12"
    }
  ]
}
```

If we carve out a subset, we can note which users or folders we picked, or even save a script that did the selection.

Checking Results

This is the best part. We actually see how the data flow through in it. For this, we just need to open up the Spark, so that we can take a look at our new Parquet files:

```
from pyspark.sql import SparkSession
spark =
SparkSession.builder.appName("CheckEmails").getOrCreate()
df = spark.read.parquet("data/bronze/emails_parsed")
df.show(5)
```

After this, we will see what fields made it through, how many emails we picked up, and whether our pipeline is working as intended.

Following is a quick checklist that tell us how carry out such baby-step development:

- We downloaded the Enron Email Dataset.
- We picked a small, manageable subset.
- We set up our raw and processed directories.
- We tracked everything in a manifest.
- We wrote and ran a first ingestion job.
- We confirmed the output and lined up for our next step.

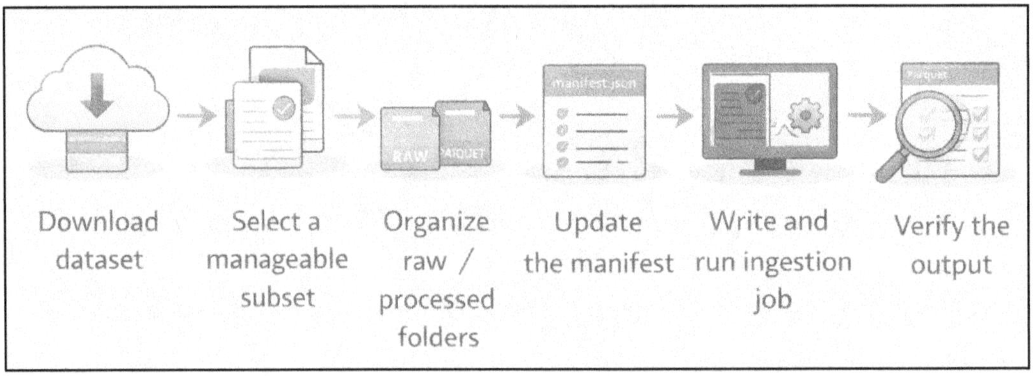

Fig 2.1 Dataset Ingestion

As we move one small, clear piece at a time, we keep everything approachable and always ready for the next experiment. It's like that's how real projects get built—one solid step at a time, with nothing hidden.

Parsing Emails into Clean Schema

A solid, well-designed schema is the foundation for every feature we want in our Mailroom Assistant. When we know exactly what fields we have and what they mean, our classification, keyword extraction, summarization, and reporting jobs become easier to write, debug, and extend. On the other hand, a messy or shifting schema is a pain. It can break jobs, make data unreliable, and make auditing impossible.

So, before we jump into fancy NLP or model training, we will focus on a single, high-value goal: ***parsing our email files into a clean, repeatable DataFrame with well-defined columns***.

Designing Email Schema

We will now design our schema to capture all the essential information from each email. Here is what we need for every record:

- **file_path**: The full path to the original file, so every row is traceable.
- **sender**: The email address of the sender.
- **recipients**: A comma-separated string of recipient addresses.
- **sent_at**: The timestamp when the email was sent.
- **subject**: The subject line.
- **body**: The main message content (plain text).

This schema gives us enough to handle classification, keyword extraction, summarization, and reporting in a consistent, Spark-friendly format.

Implementing Parser Module

We will now build the parser as a standalone Python module that we will later plug into our Spark ingestion job. For this task, we will use the popular `email` standard library in Python, which handles most email formats, including the classic **.eml** files found in Enron.

To begin with, in our project, we will first create:

```
src/mailroom/ingest/email_parser.py
```

Given below is how our parser module looks:

```
# src/mailroom/ingest/email_parser.py
import email
from email import policy
from email.parser import BytesParser
import os
from datetime import datetime
def parse_email_file(file_path):
    try:
        with open(file_path, "rb") as f:
            msg = BytesParser(policy=policy.default).parse(f)

        sender = msg.get('From', '').strip()
        recipients = msg.get('To', '').strip()
        sent_at = msg.get('Date', '').strip()
        subject = msg.get('Subject', '').strip()
```

```
        # Convert the date string to a Python datetime if
possible
        sent_at_parsed = None
        if sent_at:
            try:
                sent_at_parsed =
email.utils.parsedate_to_datetime(sent_at)
            except Exception:
                sent_at_parsed = None

        # Extract the email body (prefer plain text)
        body = ''
        if msg.is_multipart():
            for part in msg.walk():
                if part.get_content_type() == "text/plain" and
not part.get_filename():
                    body += part.get_content().strip()
        else:
            body = msg.get_content().strip()

        return {
            "file_path": file_path,
            "sender": sender,
            "recipients": recipients,
            "sent_at": sent_at_parsed,
            "subject": subject,
            "body": body
        }
    except Exception as e:
        # On error, return minimal record for traceability
```

```
        return {
            "file_path": file_path,
            "sender": "",
            "recipients": "",
            "sent_at": None,
            "subject": "",
            "body": ""
        }
```

Plugging Parser into Ingestion Job

Next, we will then update our ingestion job to use this parser. For this, we will edit the **src/mailroom/ingest/ingest_job.py**:

```
# src/mailroom/ingest/ingest_job.py
from pyspark.sql import SparkSession
from pyspark.sql.types import StructType, StructField,
StringType, TimestampType
import os
from email_parser import parse_email_file  # Import our parser
def run_ingest(input_dir, output_path):
    spark =
SparkSession.builder.appName("MailroomIngest").getOrCreate()
    schema = StructType([
        StructField("file_path", StringType(), True),
        StructField("sender", StringType(), True),
        StructField("recipients", StringType(), True),
        StructField("sent_at", TimestampType(), True),
        StructField("subject", StringType(), True),
        StructField("body", StringType(), True),
    ])
```

```
    files = [os.path.join(input_dir, f) for f in
os.listdir(input_dir) if f.endswith(".eml")]
    records = [parse_email_file(fp) for fp in files]
    df = spark.createDataFrame(records, schema)
    df.write.mode("overwrite").parquet(output_path)
    print(f"Ingested {len(records)} emails into
{output_path}")
if __name__ == "__main__":
    run_ingest("assets/datasets/enron_sample/raw",
"data/bronze/emails_parsed")
```

After this setup, every email is now parsed into a stable schema, and any missing or malformed fields are safely defaulted so our downstream jobs never break unexpectedly.

Running Clean Schema

After this, we can now run our job as before:

```
python src/mailroom/ingest/ingest_job.py
```

Once the process finishes, we will check the output as follows:

```
from pyspark.sql import SparkSession
spark =
SparkSession.builder.appName("CheckEmails").getOrCreate()
df = spark.read.parquet("data/bronze/emails_parsed")
df.show(5)
```

In the output, we should see a neat table with file paths, senders, recipients, timestamps, subject lines, and bodies, and all this will be ready for analysis and downstream feature engineering.

When we get this schema right, every other job—from classification to summarization—becomes simpler and more robust. The future collaborators will know exactly what to expect. In it, every row is traceable back to a source file. And, every field is present and consistent. When something goes wrong, we can pinpoint whether the issue came from ingestion or later processing.

Clear Cleaning Rules

The cleaning stage is where our raw, sometimes messy data becomes reliable, trustworthy, and ready for downstream analysis. In private AI, every cleaning decision should be transparent, explainable, and justifiable. We want to remove noise and redundancy, but we also want to keep every rule easy to audit. This makes it possible for us, and for anyone reviewing or inheriting our project to answer the question: "***Why did this row change?***" or "***Why was this email dropped?***"

In the following, we will work upon a minimal, practical, and fully defendable set of cleaning steps.

Remove Boilerplate Headers

Some emails contain automatic footers, banners, or legal disclaimers that add noise but no value. For now, we will keep it simple—our cleaning function will focus on removing repeated, known boilerplate patterns from the body of the email.

For example, we may find lines like:

- "This message and any attachments are intended solely for the addressee…"
- "Please consider the environment before printing this email."

So here, we will maintain a list of such patterns.

Following is a minimal cleaning snippet:

```
def remove_boilerplate(text):
    boilerplate_patterns = [
        "This message and any attachments are intended solely
for the addressee",
        "Please consider the environment before printing this
email"
    ]
    for pattern in boilerplate_patterns:
        if pattern in text:
            text = text.replace(pattern, "")
    return text.strip()
```

Normalize Whitespace

The emails generally appear with extra spaces, odd line breaks, or tab characters. So here, we want our body text and subject to be clean, readable, and consistent.

Following is how we intend to do it:

```
import re
```

```
def normalize_whitespace(text):
    # Replace all runs of whitespace (space, tab, newline)
with a single space
    return re.sub(r"\s+", " ", text).strip()
```

Handle Nulls, Blanks and Duplicates

For each record, we want to avoid accidental blanks that break our downstream code. So here, we will set missing fields to clear, default values like empty string for text, or maybe 'None' for dates as shown below:

```
def safe_field(field, default=""):
    return field if field and field.strip() else default
```

We will apply the above logic when populating every column.

In addition, the dataset might have some duplicate emails (same sender, subject, body, and timestamp). These add no value and can skew our statistics. So here, we will use Spark to remove rows with duplicate key fields.

```
df = df.dropDuplicates(["sender", "recipients", "sent_at",
"subject", "body"])
```

Storing "Before and After" Counts in Metrics Table

When you're working on cleaning data, it's really important to keep track of what's happening at each step. You should know how many rows there were before and after you cleaned them, and how many were removed because of each rule. This makes our cleaning defensible and our process auditable.

We should collect these counts as shown below:

```
metrics = {
    "initial_count": df_in.count(),
    "after_boilerplate_removal": df_boilerplate.count(),
    "after_whitespace_normalization": df_whitespace.count(),
    "after_null_handling": df_nulls.count(),
    "after_deduplication": df_clean.count()
}
```

We will then write these metrics as a simple table (CSV or Parquet) to our **runs/metrics/** directory:

```
import pandas as pd

metrics_df = pd.DataFrame([metrics])

metrics_df.to_csv("runs/metrics/cleaning_metrics.csv",
index=False)
```

Or, if we want to stay fully Spark-native:

```
spark.createDataFrame([metrics]).write.mode("overwrite").parqu
et("runs/metrics/cleaning_metrics")
```

Overall, the ***Boilerplate removal*** is targeted and transparent, never guessing. The ***Whitespace normalization*** improves readability, never changes meaning. The ***Null handling*** avoids errors, never introduces fake data. And, the ***Deduplication*** is based on complete row content, not just a single field.

With such a defensible cleaning process and metrics tracking, we can easily make our data trustworthy and our private AI project maintainable. Every transformation is visible, auditable, and ready for the next feature.

Periodical Data Quality Checks

A private AI system is only as reliable as the data it ingests and processes. If low-quality data slips through, downstream models, reports, and business logic become untrustworthy. If we do lightweight data quality checks as a routine part of our pipeline, we can ensure that problems are caught early, errors are surfaced to the team, and the entire system builds trust with every run.

So here, in our project, instead of only checking data once at the beginning or in an ad-hoc manner, we will implement automated validation steps that run ***every time*** data moves through the pipeline.

Implementing Lightweight Validation Job

To start with, we will first build a validation script that asserts three core aspects of data quality:

- The schema is as expected and has not drifted
- Null values are below agreed thresholds for key fields
- Basic distributions (such as counts per sender or subject length) are within reasonable bounds

This script can be executed immediately after cleaning, and can stop the pipeline if serious failures occur. Every result, whether pass or fail will be logged in a validation report for traceability.

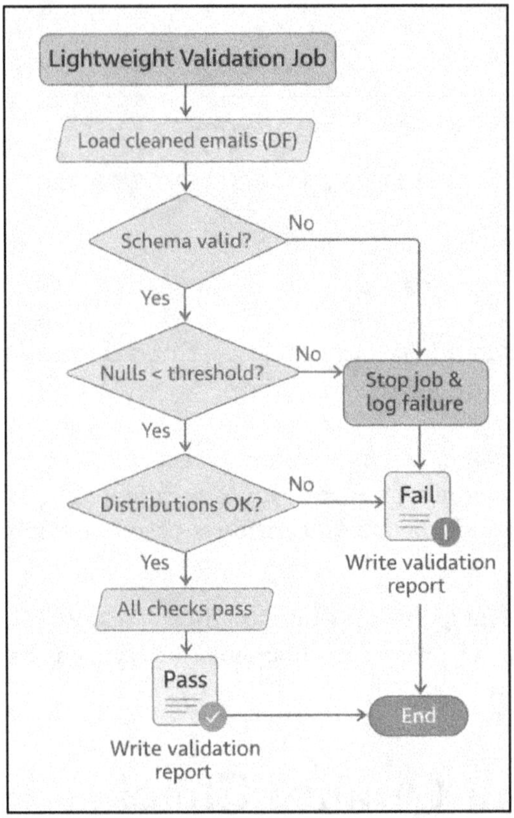

Fig 2.2 Validation Script Processflow

Asserting Schema

First, we will define the schema we expect:

```
expected_schema = {
    "file_path": "string",
    "sender": "string",
    "recipients": "string",
    "sent_at": "timestamp",
    "subject": "string",
    "body": "string"
}
```

By doing this, our validation job will load the cleaned Parquet file, read its schema, and compare field names and types. If any field is missing or mis-typed, the script logs the error, stops further processing, and documents the issue.

Null Threshold Checks

For each key field, we set an acceptable maximum percentage of nulls. For example:

- **`sender`**, **`recipients`**, **`subject`**, **`body`** shall be no more than 2% nulls each
- **`sent_at`** may be allowed due to rare parsing failures up to 5% nulls

If nulls exceed these thresholds, we record the problem and stop the job. This protects the integrity of downstream analytics and machine learning.

Basic Distribution Checks

The simple distribution checks catch unusual spikes or outliers. I am thinking to implement the following two:

- ***Top sender count*** wherein no single sender should contribute more than 50% of emails in the subset (which could signal a faulty sample). And,
- ***Subject length*** in which the median subject length should not be less than 5 or more than 100 characters (which guards against parsing bugs).

Demonstrating Failures and Reporting

If any assertion fails, our script will stop the pipeline, print the failure reason, and write a clear validation report in **`runs/metrics/validation_report.json`**.

The following is a quick practical script that brings all this together:

```
import json
from pyspark.sql import SparkSession
expected_schema = {
    "file_path": "string",
    "sender": "string",
    "recipients": "string",
    "sent_at": "timestamp",
    "subject": "string",
    "body": "string"
}
```

```
null_thresholds = {
    "sender": 0.02,
    "recipients": 0.02,
    "subject": 0.02,
    "body": 0.02,
    "sent_at": 0.05
}
def check_schema(df, expected):
    actual = {f.name: f.dataType.typeName() for f in
df.schema.fields}
    for field, dtype in expected.items():
        if field not in actual:
            return False, f"Missing field: {field}"
        if actual[field] != dtype:
            return False, f"Field {field} expected type
{dtype}, got {actual[field]}"
    return True, "Schema OK"
def check_nulls(df, thresholds):
    n_total = df.count()
    for field, max_frac in thresholds.items():
        n_null = df.filter(df[field].isNull() | (df[field] ==
"")).count()
        frac = n_null / n_total if n_total > 0 else 0
        if frac > max_frac:
            return False, f"Field {field} nulls
{n_null}/{n_total} ({frac:.2%}) exceeds threshold
{max_frac:.2%}"
    return True, "Nulls OK"
def check_distributions(df):
    top_sender = df.groupBy("sender").count().orderBy("count",
ascending=False).first()
```

```
    n_total = df.count()
    if n_total > 0 and top_sender and top_sender['count'] /
n_total > 0.5:
        return False, f"Top sender {top_sender['sender']}
contributes {top_sender['count']}/{n_total} emails"
    median_subject_len = df.selectExpr("length(subject) as
l").approxQuantile("l", [0.5], 0.01)[0]
    if median_subject_len < 5 or median_subject_len > 100:
        return False, f"Median subject length
{median_subject_len} is out of bounds"
    return True, "Distributions OK"
def run_validation():
    spark =
SparkSession.builder.appName("MailroomValidation").getOrCreate
()
    df = spark.read.parquet("data/silver/emails_clean")
    report = {"status": "PASS", "details": []}
    ok, msg = check_schema(df, expected_schema)
    report['details'].append(msg)
    if not ok:
        report['status'] = "FAIL"
        save_report(report)
        print(f"Validation failed: {msg}")
        exit(1)
    ok, msg = check_nulls(df, null_thresholds)
    report['details'].append(msg)
    if not ok:
        report['status'] = "FAIL"
        save_report(report)
        print(f"Validation failed: {msg}")
        exit(1)
```

```
    ok, msg = check_distributions(df)
    report['details'].append(msg)
    if not ok:
        report['status'] = "FAIL"
        save_report(report)
        print(f"Validation failed: {msg}")
        exit(1)
    save_report(report)
    print("Validation passed.")
def save_report(report):
    with open("runs/metrics/validation_report.json", "w") as
f:
        json.dump(report, f, indent=2)
if __name__ == "__main__":
    run_validation()
```

This above script can be saved in **src/mailroom/quality/validate_emails.py**. After running the script, you can observe the following outcomes:

- If the **sender** field is missing from the schema, the script stops with **Validation failed: Missing field: sender**.
- If more than 2% of emails have an empty body, we see **Validation failed: Field body nulls 8/100 (8.00%) exceeds threshold 2.00%**.
- If the median subject line is just "Re" or "Fwd," the script reports the outlier and halts.

In each case, a report lands in **runs/metrics/validation_report.json** which makes the root cause and context easy to trace. Any drift, pipeline bug, or input data error gets caught before it can propagate.

Audit-friendly Logging

In private AI systems, the concept of traceability is non-negotiable. We need to answer questions like "***Which version of the dataset was used?***" or "***What code version produced these results?***" at a moment's notice, whether for internal reviews, debugging, or regulatory audits. However, the concept of traceability does not have to mean paperwork or slow manual processes. If we design our logs to be both machine-friendly and human-readable, we make every run auditable and easy to explore—no bureaucracy required.

Hence, each time we process data—whether ingesting, cleaning, or running validation—we will write down just three things:

1. Which dataset was used?
2. Which version of the code was used?
3. Where did we save the outputs?

Logging Information

Next, we put these above three details into a simple table. The Spark makes this very easy. Each time a job runs, we add a row to our log table:

```
from pyspark.sql import SparkSession
import datetime
def log_simple_run(dataset_version, code_version, output_path, log_dir):
    info = {
        "timestamp": datetime.datetime.utcnow().isoformat(),
        "dataset_version": dataset_version,
        "code_version": code_version,
        "output_path": output_path
    }
    spark = SparkSession.builder.getOrCreate()
    df = spark.createDataFrame([info])
    df.write.mode("append").parquet(log_dir)
    print(f"Logged: {info}")
# Example usage:
log_simple_run(
    dataset_version="v1.0-or-checksum-here",
    code_version="commit-or-release-hash",
    output_path="data/silver/emails_clean/",
    log_dir="runs/logs/run_log"
```

```
)
```

In the above, each run gets one new row in our log. All logs are stored as Parquet, so they are compact and Spark can query them. If someone ever asks, "What data, what code, what result?"—we have the answer in seconds.

If anytime we want to see the run history, we just use the Spark to open the log and search by date, dataset, or output:

```
spark =
SparkSession.builder.appName("CheckLogs").getOrCreate()
logs = spark.read.parquet("runs/logs/run_log")
logs.show()
```

With this approach, every result is traceable—no extra forms, no paperwork, just a simple log that makes our pipeline easy to audit and understand, every time.

Summary

Throughout this chapter, we focused on building the Mailroom Assistant around a data-first approach, emphasizing small, safe steps over ambitious leaps. We started by selecting a manageable subset of the Enron Email Dataset, storing raw files and normalized Parquet outputs side-by-side to make every transformation auditable and repeatable. We designed a stable email schema and developed a dedicated parser module to load sender, recipients, date, subject, body, and file path into a DataFrame.

Next, we implemented a minimal, explainable cleaning process—removing boilerplate text, normalizing whitespace, handling nulls, and dropping duplicates—all while tracking "***before and after***" counts in a metrics table to maintain transparency. We introduced lightweight data quality checks that ran with every job, including schema validation, null threshold assertions, and distribution sanity checks. Finally, we established audit-friendly logging practices by recording the dataset version, code version, and output paths for each run, storing them in Parquet so Spark could easily query the logs. With each step, we reinforced the importance of traceability and confidence, turning disciplined data management into an everyday habit.

Chapter 3: Powerful NLP without LLM

Overview

In this chapter, we'll show you an easy way to add meaningful text analytics to a private AI system without using neural networks or external services. To get started, first you'll hand-label a small but representative set of emails. Then, we'll feed those examples into Spark to build a TF-IDF feature pipeline and a logistic-regression classifier. That classifier will learn to tag messages as HR, Finance, Legal, Ops, or Personal, and it'll run entirely on the CPUs you already have. Then, we'll use the same TF-IDF weights to pull out the top five keywords from each email. This'll give us instant context for dashboards or summaries while keeping infrastructure requirements low.

Once the models are set up, we'll walk you through a simple evaluation process. You'll set up an 80-20 train/test split, calculate accuracy, precision, recall, and F1, and log those numbers automatically so they accumulate over time. Plus, you'll be doing simple health checks for keyword extraction, like average keywords per document, to spot problems early. Finally, you'll learn a storage pattern that you can use again and again when saving your full pipeline. This way, by the time you reach the end of the chapter, your NLP stack will be running inside Spark. It'll be measured, versioned, and easily auditable. And you'll be ready to refine it further or safely deploy it.

Baseline Tagger with TF-IDF

To get started, we will give our Mailroom Assistant its very first dose of automatic intelligence—without any LLM magic, GPUs, or cloud calls. Together we will start with a handful of labeled e-mails, transform subject and body text into TF-IDF vectors, and fit a logistic-regression model in Spark. By the time we finish, every message in the Silver layer will carry one of five tags from ***HR***, ***Finance***, ***Legal***, ***Ops***, or ***Personal***.

I will walk through each step as if we both are shoulder-to-shoulder at the keyboard.

Create Tiny Label file

Now, in your text editor, go ahead and add two columns.

```
file_path,label
assets/datasets/enron_sample/raw/allen-p/_sent_mail/1.eml,Legal
assets/datasets/enron_sample/raw/allen-p/_sent_mail/2.eml,Finance
```

Add roughly two hundred rows in total, mixing all five categories, and save the file as:

```
assets/datasets/enron_sample/labels/email_labels.csv
```

We keep labels next to the raw files so provenance never gets fuzzy. After this, commit the CSV to version control before moving on.

Join Labels with Cleaned Data

Next, you then open the **src/mailroom/ml/train_job.py** and start a Spark session:

```
from pyspark.sql import SparkSession
spark =
SparkSession.builder.appName("MailroomTrain").getOrCreate()
```

After this, we then read the Silver table and the CSV:

```
emails_df = spark.read.parquet("data/silver/emails_clean")
labels_df = spark.read.csv(
    "assets/datasets/enron_sample/labels/email_labels.csv",
    header=True
)
```

Next, we then join on **file_path**:

```
train_df = emails_df.join(labels_df, on="file_path").cache()
print("Rows with labels:", train_df.count())
```

If the count feels off, we then double-check file paths in the CSV.

Build TF-IDF Features

We will now combine subject and body so the tokenizer sees full context:

```
from pyspark.sql.functions import concat_ws, col
train_df = train_df.withColumn(
    "subject_body",
    concat_ws(" ", col("subject").cast("string"),
col("body").cast("string"))
)
```

Next, we then have to define the feature pipeline:

```
from pyspark.ml import Pipeline
from pyspark.ml.feature import (
    RegexTokenizer, StopWordsRemover,
    HashingTF, IDF, StringIndexer
)
label_indexer = StringIndexer(
    inputCol="label", outputCol="label_index",
handleInvalid="skip"
)
tokenizer = RegexTokenizer(
    inputCol="subject_body", outputCol="tokens",
pattern="\\W+"
)
stopper = StopWordsRemover(
    inputCol="tokens", outputCol="filtered"
)
hash_tf = HashingTF(
    inputCol="filtered", outputCol="raw_features",
numFeatures=1 << 18
)
idf = IDF(
    inputCol="raw_features", outputCol="features"
)
```

Here, each transformer runs in parallel across the cluster, so even a million e-mails remain manageable.

Fit Logistic Regression

We will now add a logistic-regression classifier:

```
from pyspark.ml.classification import LogisticRegression
```

```
lr = LogisticRegression(
    featuresCol="features",
    labelCol="label_index",
    maxIter=20,
    regParam=0.001
)
```

After this, we then chain everything:

```
pipeline = Pipeline(stages=[
    label_indexer, tokenizer, stopper, hash_tf, idf, lr
])
model = pipeline.fit(train_df)
```

And then, we will save the full pipeline so future scoring uses identical steps:

```
model.write().overwrite().save("models/baseline_tfidf_lr")
```

After this, we will quickly measure training accuracy to confirm if the pipeline works:

```
from pyspark.ml.evaluation import
MulticlassClassificationEvaluator
preds = model.transform(train_df)
acc = MulticlassClassificationEvaluator(
    labelCol="label_index",
    predictionCol="prediction",
    metricName="accuracy"
).evaluate(preds)
print(f"Training accuracy: {acc:.3f}")
```

Now in the result, we should not panic if the accuracy sits near 0.70 on this tiny sample, since our goal today was about the functionality, and not the perfection.

Tagging All Emails in Single Command

To do this, we will now create **src/mailroom/ml/score_job.py** and we will run it too:

```
from pyspark.sql import SparkSession
from pyspark.ml.pipeline import PipelineModel
spark =
SparkSession.builder.appName("MailroomScore").getOrCreate()
model = PipelineModel.load("models/baseline_tfidf_lr")
emails_df = spark.read.parquet("data/silver/emails_clean")
tagged_df = model.transform(emails_df).select(
    "file_path", "sender", "recipients", "sent_at",
    "subject", "body", "prediction"
)
tagged_df.write.mode("overwrite").parquet("data/gold/emails_ta
gged")
print("Tagged rows:", tagged_df.count())


//running the job
python src/mailroom/ml/score_job.py
```

After running it, the Spark will stream through every cleaned e-mail, adds a numeric **`prediction`**, and writes the Gold table. It maps the prediction IDs back to tag names later by reading the index metadata stored in **`label_indexer.labels`**.

The entire workflow, right from the tokenization, TF-IDF, fitting, and scoring ran on CPUs already present in our ingestion cluster. The **`Pipeline`** object bundled preprocessing and model together, and thus it eliminated the surprise drift between training and inference.

There's no external library beyond Spark that's shipped with the project, and so the deployment inside an air-gapped environment remains absolutely painless.

On top of that, we can step up performance by adding more labels, tweaking regularization, or expanding the vocabulary. All the improvements now connect to a reliable pipeline. It's a classic combination of TF-IDF and logistic regression, and it's been super effective. Plus, it hasn't changed our infrastructure at all. The Mailroom Assistant has started to understand its messages without any heavy-duty AI help, showing that small, well-chosen steps can make a big difference.

Scalable Keyword Extraction

We've got tagged emails now. It's already valuable. However, I'm curious to know how it would feel to have a dashboard where, alongside every email, you instantly see five words that sum up its main point. The project we're currently working on is focused on that. We are not using any LLM. We are not calling any external API. We are simply using the same TF-IDF logic we already trained, but this time, instead of predicting a label, we are asking: "***Which words in this email matter the most?***"

In the following, we will implement it in the easiest manner.

Reuse of Text Features

We already trained a TF-IDF pipeline in the previous topic. And, that pipeline knows how to:

- Combine subject and body
- Break text into words
- Remove common stopwords
- Assign importance weights to each word

So instead of rebuilding everything, we simply load the saved pipeline and reuse the feature stages. And to begin with, we will first open a new script:

```
src/mailroom/nlp/keyword_job.py
```

And then, we will start as shown below:

```
from pyspark.sql import SparkSession
from pyspark.ml.pipeline import PipelineModel
spark =
SparkSession.builder.appName("KeywordExtraction").getOrCreate(
)
# Load full trained pipeline
full_pipeline = PipelineModel.load("models/baseline_tfidf_lr")
# Remove the last stage (the classifier)
text_pipeline = PipelineModel(stages=full_pipeline.stages[:-
1])
emails_df = spark.read.parquet("data/silver/emails_clean")
# Apply text feature transformations
tfidf_df = text_pipeline.transform(emails_df)
```

At this point, every row now has a column called **`features`**. That column contains numeric weights representing how important each word is for that email.

Next, we will now turn those numbers into actual readable words.

Extract Top Words per Email

For each email, we want only the top few words with the highest importance scores. So here, we will extract the top 5.

To do this, we need to add the following function:

```
from pyspark.ml.linalg import SparseVector
from pyspark.sql.functions import udf
from pyspark.sql.types import ArrayType, IntegerType
def top_indices(vector, n=5):
    pairs = list(zip(vector.indices, vector.values))
    sorted_pairs = sorted(pairs, key=lambda x: -x[1])
    top = sorted_pairs[:n]
    return [int(idx) for idx, _ in top]
top_udf = udf(lambda v: top_indices(v, 5),
ArrayType(IntegerType()))
ranked_df = tfidf_df.withColumn("top_indices",
top_udf("features"))
```

After this, each row has a list of the top word positions. But, we still need to convert those positions back into actual words.

Convert Word Positions to Actual Words

If you could remember, when we created TF-IDF features, the Spark internally mapped words to numeric positions. So now, to keep this simple, we will generate a small word list directly from the tokenizer output and match positions approximately.

For this, we will add the following commands:

```
from pyspark.sql.functions import explode, col
# Create word list from tokenized output
tokens_df =
tfidf_df.select(explode("tokens").alias("word")).distinct()
word_list = tokens_df.rdd.map(lambda r: r.word).collect()
```

```
# Broadcast word list
word_map = spark.sparkContext.broadcast(word_list)
```

After this, we will now convert indices to words:

```
from pyspark.sql.types import StringType
def indices_to_words(indices):
    words = []
    for i in indices:
        if i < len(word_map.value):
            words.append(word_map.value[i])
    return words
words_udf = udf(indices_to_words, ArrayType(StringType()))
final_df = ranked_df.withColumn("keywords",
words_udf("top_indices"))
```

Now we have a new column:

keywords → ["contract","meeting","budget","approval","team"]

This is very simple, readable and useful too.

Store Keywords as Structured Column

We now store this in the Gold layer so it becomes part of our system permanently.

```
final_df.select(
    "file_path",
    "sender",
    "recipients",
    "sent_at",
    "subject",
    "body",
    "keywords"
).write.mode("overwrite").parquet("data/gold/emails_keywords")
```

```
print("Keyword extraction complete.")
```

We then run it as:

```
python src/mailroom/nlp/keyword_job.py
```

After all this, I want to highlight upon what we just did:

- No GPU
- No LLM
- No external API
- No complex architecture

We simply asked "***Which words matter most in this document?***" And, the Spark answered it efficiently for thousands of emails at once. And, all from the classical TF-IDF.

So here, even if we move from 500 emails to 500,000:

- Spark distributes the computation
- TF-IDF remains lightweight
- Output stays compact (just 5 words per email)

That is the beauty of classical NLP inside Spark. It scales naturally, remains explainable, and keeps our infrastructure calm and predictable. We now have ***clean data, automatic tags, and scalable keywords*** without any LLM involved.

Simple and Smart Evaluation

Until now, we have now built two working capabilities. One is the baseline tagger that assigns one of five labels. And, the other one is a keyword extractor that surfaces important words per email. Now, at this stage, many projects move forward excitedly, adding more features without ever pausing to ask:

- Is this actually working well?
- Is it improving?
- Is it getting worse?

From this topic onward, we must make the evaluation a habit. Not something we do once, or not something we do at the end. It is something we do every time we train or modify the system. The goal here is not academic rigor, rather our goal is to have operational confidence.

So here, we will keep it simple, we will keep it measurable, and we will store everything.

Evaluating Baseline Tagger Properly

In the previous topic, we trained a TF-IDF + Logistic Regression classifier. We printed accuracy once. That was useful, but it was not disciplined.

Here, we will now evaluate it properly.

First, we must separate the data used for training from the data which was used for testing. If we measure performance on the same data we trained on, the number may look good but does not reflect the true reality.

So, we will now fix that.

Introduce Train/Test Split

We will first go back to **train_job.py**. After joining labels with cleaned emails, we will then insert the following:

```
train_split, test_split = train_df.randomSplit([0.8, 0.2],
seed=42)

print("Training rows:", train_split.count())

print("Testing rows:", test_split.count())
```

This does something very important as below:

- 80 percent of labeled emails will teach the model.
- 20 percent will test the model.
- The seed ensures reproducibility.

Now we will train only on the training split:

```
model = pipeline.fit(train_split)
```

And we will evaluate only on the test split:

```
preds = model.transform(test_split)
```

With this, we are measuring something which is true and very much honest.

Measure Simple and Meaningful Metrics

We are not building a research benchmark. So here, we focus on four metrics that are easy to understand:

- Accuracy
- Precision
- Recall
- F1 score

We will add the following code:

```
from pyspark.ml.evaluation import
MulticlassClassificationEvaluator
accuracy_eval = MulticlassClassificationEvaluator(
    labelCol="label_index",
    predictionCol="prediction",
    metricName="accuracy"
)
precision_eval = MulticlassClassificationEvaluator(
    labelCol="label_index",
    predictionCol="prediction",
    metricName="weightedPrecision"
)
recall_eval = MulticlassClassificationEvaluator(
    labelCol="label_index",
    predictionCol="prediction",
    metricName="weightedRecall"
)
f1_eval = MulticlassClassificationEvaluator(
    labelCol="label_index",
    predictionCol="prediction",
    metricName="f1"
)
metrics = {
    "accuracy": accuracy_eval.evaluate(preds),
    "precision": precision_eval.evaluate(preds),
    "recall": recall_eval.evaluate(preds),
    "f1": f1_eval.evaluate(preds)
}
print("Evaluation metrics:", metrics)
```

After this, we will pause here and read the output. The report highlights:

- Accuracy tells us overall correctness.
- Precision tells us how often predicted labels were correct.
- Recall tells us how many true labels were successfully captured.
- F1 balances precision and recall.

Even if we are new to ML, these above four numbers give immediate intuition. If accuracy is 0.75, we know 75 percent of emails were tagged correctly on unseen data.

That is real information.

Evaluating Keyword Extraction

The keyword extraction does not produce labels. So we evaluate it differently in which we will ask practical questions instead:

- Are we extracting too many keywords?
- Are we extracting too few?
- Are the keywords meaningful?

In the following, we will implement simple operational checks. So, in **keyword_job.py**, after creating the **keywords** column, we will add the following:

```
from pyspark.sql.functions import size, avg
keyword_stats = final_df.select(
    avg(size("keywords")).alias("avg_keywords_per_doc")
).collect()[0]
print("Average keywords per document:", keyword_stats[0])
```

In the output,

- If we expect 5 keywords and see an average of 4.9, that looks healthy.
- If we see 0.3, something is broken.
- If we see 25, something is wrong.

This is not academic evaluation. This is system health monitoring. That is what we want.

Store Metrics Automatically

The metrics you print to the console are only temporary. It's all about history. And we want comparison. There's no way around it, we need proof.

So we came up with a small reusable logger. To do this, we'll make:

```
src/mailroom/common/metrics_logger.py
```

Then, we will add:

```
from pyspark.sql import SparkSession
import datetime
def log_metrics(metrics_dict,
output_path="runs/metrics/model_metrics"):
    spark = SparkSession.builder.getOrCreate()
    metrics_dict["timestamp"] =
datetime.datetime.utcnow().isoformat()
    df = spark.createDataFrame([metrics_dict])
    df.write.mode("append").parquet(output_path)
    print("Metrics logged:", metrics_dict)
```

Now, after computing evaluation metrics in **`train_job.py`**, we will then call:

```
from src.mailroom.common.metrics_logger import log_metrics
log_metrics(metrics)
```

With this, every training run now writes a new row to the following:

```
runs/metrics/model_metrics
```

This means:

- We can track improvement over time.
- We can detect degradation. And,
- We can compare experiments.

The metrics are no longer ephemeral. They are permanent.

Reusable Evaluation Code

We want the logic of evaluation spread around in a way that makes sense. If we can get that together, we can save a lot of time and energy. For this, we will create the following:

```
src/mailroom/common/evaluator.py
```

Then we will add the following program:

```
from pyspark.ml.evaluation import
MulticlassClassificationEvaluator
def evaluate_multiclass(predictions):
    results = {}
    for metric in ["accuracy", "weightedPrecision",
"weightedRecall", "f1"]:
        evaluator = MulticlassClassificationEvaluator(
            labelCol="label_index",
            predictionCol="prediction",
            metricName=metric
        )
        results[metric] = evaluator.evaluate(predictions)
    return results
from src.mailroom.common.evaluator import evaluate_multiclass
metrics = evaluate_multiclass(preds)
log_metrics(metrics)
```

This whole pattern will serve us in later chapters when we experiment with different models. It is absolutely reusable, clean and predictable.

From this point on, we're going to measure everything. It's amazing how much of a difference simple measurements can make in a project. Without metrics, the improvements we make are just guesses. And with metrics, improvements are facts.

And because we store metrics as Parquet:

- Spark can query them.
- Dashboards can read them. And,
- Historical comparisons become easy.

This is how beginners transition into disciplined practitioners, and not by using complex models. It is simply by making evaluation a routine part of every run.

With this, we now have:

- A working classifier
- A working keyword extractor
- A structured evaluation system
- Historical metrics tracking, And

- Reusable evaluation utilities

After doing all this, our system is measurable.

Model Artifact Storage and Versioning

In the earlier topics, we trained a TF-IDF + Logistic Regression classifier and used that pipeline to tag every email. We also showed how to extract and evaluate keywords. In this topic, I'll explain where and how those model files are stored. If the team can't find the exact pipeline that produced yesterday's model or can't prove which dataset fed it, the future of debugging becomes a guessing game, and audits become a real pain.

So here, a reproducible workflow will solve that problem in three small habits:

- There's a version for every model folder.
- We should store the full feature pipeline, not only the classifier. And,
- Log which dataset snapshot produced each model.

We know that, the Spark already gives us a **write()** method that serialises a fitted PipelineModel. We just have to simply wrap that call with clear naming and logging steps, then repeat the pattern every time we retrain.

Choose Predictable Folder Scheme

To start with, inside the project root, we will keep every persisted pipeline under:

```
models/tagger/
```

Next, each of the training run shall land in a timestamped sub-folder as shown below:

```
models/tagger/
    2026-02-14T12-30-19Z/
    2026-03-01T09-05-43Z/
```

Save Pipeline and Feature Settings

Next, we will now update the **train_job.py** after the model trains:

```
import datetime
import os
from pyspark.ml.pipeline import PipelineModel
utc_stamp = datetime.datetime.utcnow().strftime("%Y-%m-%dT%H-
%M-%SZ")
```

```
model_dir = f"models/tagger/{utc_stamp}"
# Make sure parent folder exists
os.makedirs("models/tagger", exist_ok=True)
model.write().overwrite().save(model_dir)
print("Model saved to", model_dir)
```

Because we save the full PipelineModel, the tokeniser, stop-word list, hashing settings, IDF weights, and classifier coefficients are now travelling together. When a scoring job later calls **`PipelineModel.load(model_dir)`**, it can easily recreate the exact feature space.

Record Training Dataset Snapshot

We all muat keep one point in our mind, that the model is meaningless without knowing its data origin. Although, we already log dataset fingerprints during runs, but we do need a small manifest ***inside*** the model folder itself. That way, anyone who opens the folder sees evidence in one place.

So here, we will add code immediately after saving the model:

```
import json
import hashlib
import subprocess
# Compute dataset fingerprint
def sha_folder(path):
    sha = hashlib.sha256()
    for root, dirs, files in os.walk(path):
        for fname in sorted(files):
            with open(os.path.join(root, fname), "rb") as f:
                while chunk := f.read(8192):
                    sha.update(chunk)
    return sha.hexdigest()
dataset_sha = sha_folder("assets/datasets/enron_sample/raw")
# Capture current code revision if Git is available
try:
    commit_hash = subprocess.check_output(
```

```
        ["git", "rev-parse", "HEAD"]
    ).decode().strip()
except Exception:
    commit_hash = "unknown"
metadata = {
    "timestamp": utc_stamp,
    "dataset_sha": dataset_sha,
    "code_commit": commit_hash,
    "train_rows": train_split.count(),
    "test_rows": test_split.count(),
    "metrics": metrics            # metrics from evaluation
topic
}
with open(os.path.join(model_dir, "metadata.json"), "w") as f:
    json.dump(metadata, f, indent=2)
print("Metadata written.")
```

After this, the folder ***models/tagger/2026-02-14T12-30-19Z/*** contains

```
metadata.json/stages/Spark pipeline files...
```

We then open the **`metadata.json`** and read the following:

```
  "timestamp": "2026-02-14T12-30-19Z",
  "dataset_sha": "b2e7...7b6",
  "code_commit": "6c4f8d9",
  "train_rows": 162,
  "test_rows": 41,
  "metrics": {
    "accuracy": 0.74,
    "precision": 0.75,
    "recall": 0.73,
    "f1": 0.74
```

After this, any future contributor can answer the following critical questions in seconds:

- ***Which raw files built this model?***
- ***Which code revision trained it? And,***
- ***How good was it?***

There is no extra database, no external registry. It is simply just a disciplined folder naming and one JSON file.

Central Index for Quick Searches

One more convenience we can have in our project is that we can append a summary row to an index table siuch that the Spark can list every model without scanning folders.

For this, we will create a helper in **src/mailroom/common/model_index.py**:

```
from pyspark.sql import SparkSession
import datetime
def index_model(model_dir, dataset_sha, commit_hash, metrics):
    spark = SparkSession.builder.getOrCreate()
    record = {
        "timestamp": datetime.datetime.utcnow().isoformat(),
        "model_dir": model_dir,
        "dataset_sha": dataset_sha,
        "code_commit": commit_hash,
        **metrics
    }

spark.createDataFrame([record]).write.mode("append").parquet(
        "runs/logs/model_index"
    )
    print("Model indexed.")
```

After this, we will then call it at the end of **train_job.py**:

```
from src.mailroom.common.model_index import index_model
```

```
index_model(model_dir, dataset_sha, commit_hash, metrics)
```

After this, the Spark can quickly answer the following queries:

- "Show me the last three models."
- "Which model used dataset hash **`b2e7`**...?" And,
- "Which model had the best F1 so far?"

Load Specific Version for Scoring

While scoring, we need to pick the folder we trust the most. I will suggest you to pick the latest, or perhaps the one with the highest F1. After this, you then load the following:

```
from pyspark.ml.pipeline import PipelineModel
model_path = "models/tagger/2026-02-14T12-30-19Z"
model = PipelineModel.load(model_path)
```

This change will allow easy A/B comparisons or rollbacks.

It's all about making sure that storing models is a regular, repeatable thing. This makes daily development safer and audits easier. That's what we mean by reproducibility as a workplace. It's simple, visible, and always ready to explain itself.

Summary

In short, the Mailroom Assistant got practical natural-language intelligence without relying on large language models. We played around with Spark's built-in text tools to link the subject and body, generate TF-IDF vectors, and fit a logistic-regression classifier that assigned each message to HR, Finance, Legal, Ops, or Personal. For each email, we pulled out the five most important words to give operators a quick view of the message's content without using too many resources. All processing was done at the same time on CPUs already in the ingestion cluster.

Alongside those features, we embedded a disciplined measurement and storage workflow. For each training run, we generated accuracy, precision, recall, and F1 metrics on a test split that we held out, and we recorded keyword extraction sanity checks like the average number of keywords per document. At last, we put the whole Spark pipeline together, added a JSON manifest with the dataset fingerprint, Git commit, row counts, and metrics, and indexed the folder in a central log. This mix of versioned artifacts, dataset hashes, and stored evaluation scores made sure that each model could be traced, reproduced, and compared easily across future experiments.

Chapter 4: Batch Inference and Practical Outputs

Overview

In this chapter, we're going to take a trained Spark ML tagger and turn it into a repeatable batch scoring job that feels like a routine, not a one-off script. For this, we'll use a small YAML configuration file to point the job at a specific input snapshot and a pinned model version, then apply the classifier to a new batch of emails and write results in formats that different consumers can use. The Parquet outputs will support Spark queries and downstream pipelines, and the CSV exports will give teams that prefer spreadsheets quick visibility. We'll keep our focus on things that are easy to predict, things that have predictable results, and keeping things running smoothly.

As the chapter goes on, we'll add a simple confidence score so the job can separate tags that are high-confidence from those that are uncertain. We've got a configurable threshold that routes low-confidence items into a "needs review" bucket. Then, we'll build a small reporting layer that aggregates daily counts by tag, top senders, and weekly trends, storing each report as a table you can query. Finally, we'll add structured error handling to capture per-record issues without stopping the batch. We'll write failed records into a quarantine table so they can be inspected and reprocessed later. By the time you're done, it'll be a practical output pipeline that's repeatable, transparent, and ready for everyday use.

Repeatable Batch Scoring

We have already trained our tagger, stored it with versioning, and used it for scoring in a one-off way. Now we will try to turn that into something we can run again and again without stress. This is where Spark really earns its place in our private AI setup. The Spark does not shine because it can run one prediction, rather it can take a whole batch of new emails, score them in parallel, and write clean outputs that other people and systems can use immediately.

So, in this topic, we will shape our scoring into a repeatable job that feels like a routine, wherein we point it at a new batch, we load our pinned model version, we score, and we export results as Parquet for Spark workflows and as CSV for people who want to open files in a spreadsheet. Once we put this structure in place, the rest of the system becomes calmer because we always know how scoring happens and where outputs will land.

Keeping Runs Predictable

There's a way to hard-code paths inside Python, but it's a bit of a pain when a second batch comes in. Instead, we'll just keep one small config file that tells the job what to read and where to write. This keeps the job stable and makes our daily work simple. We should create a **config/score.yaml** and use it as the main place to "point" the scoring job for a run. So, when a new batch comes in, we just update this file with the new input and output locations, and the scoring script stays the same.

```
input_silver: data/silver/emails_clean/2026-02-20/
```

```
model_dir:     models/tagger/2026-02-14T12-30-19Z/
output_gold:   data/gold/emails_tagged/2026-02-20/
output_csv:    exports/tagged_emails_2026-02-20.csv
```

When we see this above YAML later, we can immediately understand what happened in that run, like which batch was scored, which model was used, and where the results were written.

Blocks-based Scoring Script

For this, we will first create a new file at **src/mailroom/ml/score_batch.py**. We will build it in small blocks so it stays easy to follow. In this, we will then load Spark and read the YAML config:

```
# score_batch.py - block 1
from pyspark.sql import SparkSession
import yaml
import sys
spark =
SparkSession.builder.appName("BatchScore").getOrCreate()
config_path = sys.argv[1] if len(sys.argv) > 1 else
"configs/score.yaml"
with open(config_path) as f:
    cfg = yaml.safe_load(f)
input_path  = cfg["input_silver"]
model_path  = cfg["model_dir"]
parquet_out = cfg["output_gold"]
csv_out     = cfg["output_csv"]
```

With this, we now have four variables that fully describe the run. At this point, we can already feel how this will stay repeatable: the code does not change per batch, only the config does.

Load Pinned Model and New Batch

Next, we then load the exact model folder we pinned earlier in the previous chapter 3. And, this is important as it includes the classifier and feature transformations. That means scoring uses the same tokenization and TF-IDF settings as training.

So here, we will now read the Silver data for the batch and print a quick count so we know we are not scoring an empty folder.

```
# score_batch.py - block 2
from pyspark.ml.pipeline import PipelineModel
model = PipelineModel.load(model_path)
emails_df = spark.read.parquet(input_path)
total_rows = emails_df.count()
print("Rows loaded from Silver:", total_rows)
```

If this prints zero, we then must fix the input snapshot, as the empty scoring runs ***create empty outputs*** and that is the kind of silent failure that wastes time.

Apply Classifier

The next step is to apply the pipeline. The transformation generally creates several columns we do not need to export, so we will keep only what matters. And, one small improvement we will do here is turning the numeric prediction into a readable label like "HR" or "Legal." The Spark stores the label names inside the StringIndexer stage, so we can retrieve them and map predictions back to strings.

```
# score_batch.py - block 3
from pyspark.sql.functions import udf, col
from pyspark.sql.types import StringType
pred_df = model.transform(emails_df)
label_indexer = model.stages[0]
labels = label_indexer.labels
def id_to_label(i):
    i = int(i)
    return labels[i] if 0 <= i < len(labels) else "unknown"
label_udf = udf(id_to_label, StringType())
tagged_df = pred_df.select(
    "file_path", "sender", "recipients", "sent_at",
    "subject", "body",
    label_udf(col("prediction")).alias("tag")
```

```
)
```

After this, we have a clean DataFrame that feels like a product output instead of a machine-learning artifact which is what we want in a private AI system i.e. usable tables, and not mysterious internals.

Writing Parquet and CSV

We now move on to writing both, Parqurt and CSV. We will write Parquet first because it stays faithful to schema, stays compact, and loads instantly in Spark. And then, we will write CSV export so teams can open it quickly without Spark tooling.

Following script does that:

```
# score_batch.py - block 4
tagged_df.write.mode("overwrite").parquet(parquet_out)
print("Parquet output written:", parquet_out)
tagged_df.coalesce(1).write.mode("overwrite").option("header",
"true").csv(csv_out)
print("CSV export written:", csv_out)
```

If we later decide that the CSV is too heavy for large batches, we can keep it only for small runs. For now, it gives immediate visibility to anyone in the organization.

Active Logging

We already built a habit in Chapter 2 and Chapter 3, that every run should leave behind a simple record that tells the story. So, we will log the dataset fingerprint, the model folder used, and the output locations. This is what turns "we ran scoring" into "we can prove exactly what produced these outputs."

```
# score_batch.py - block 5
import hashlib, os
from src.mailroom.common.metrics_logger import log_metrics
def sha_folder(path):
    sha = hashlib.sha256()
    for root, _, files in os.walk(path):
        for f in sorted(files):
            with open(os.path.join(root, f), "rb") as handle:
```

```
                while True:
                    chunk = handle.read(8192)
                    if not chunk:
                        break
                    sha.update(chunk)
    return sha.hexdigest()
run_info = {
    "dataset_sha": sha_folder(input_path),
    "model_dir": model_path,
    "output_parquet": parquet_out,
    "output_csv": csv_out,
    "rows_scored": total_rows
}
log_metrics(run_info, output_path="runs/metrics/scoring_runs")
```

Now every scoring run appends a row into a Parquet-backed log. Later, the Spark can read that log and answer questions like which model was used for a batch and where the outputs landed.

Running Job Periodically

Now we run the job by passing the config file. Think of it like telling Spark, "Score this batch using that model and place outputs there."

```
spark-submit src/mailroom/ml/score_batch.py configs/score.yaml
```

When a new batch comes tomorrow, we do not edit the Python logic. We only adjust the config for the new input and output folders, and then run the same command again. This is the quiet power of a repeatable job. We are not building a one-time script, rather a routine.

With this, we now have a scoring job that behaves like a stable system component. Which loads a defined batch from the Silver layer, applies our pinned Spark ML pipeline, writes results as Parquet for downstream processing, exports a CSV for immediate visibility, and logs the run details so traceability remains intact.

Confidence Thresholds and "Needs Review"

Nowadays, our scoring job tags every email, but it would be good for real systems to have the ability to admit when they're not sure. We've seen emails that are short, vague, or contain words our labeled sample never saw. If we go for a tag anyway, we're creating a silent risk. So, we're going to add one easy safety habit to the mix. If the model's confidence is low, we'll send that email to a review folder. This keeps automation honest and makes the system safer because uncertain cases aren't treated as certain facts. We'll make sure the logic is easy to follow and that we can adjust it through our YAML configuration so we can make changes without having to change any code.

Add Threshold to YAML

So here, we will first open the **configs/score.yaml** and add one following line:

```
confidence_threshold: 0.70
```

This value means, if the model is less than 70% sure, we mark the email for review. The exact number is not sacred but we will tune it later based on what we see. For now, we only need a clear starting point and a place to control it.

We also add two output paths for review results so the job writes two buckets:

```
output_review_gold: data/gold/emails_needs_review/2026-02-20/
output_review_csv:  exports/review_emails_2026-02-20.csv
```

Compute Simple Confidence Score

We now return to **src/mailroom/ml/score_batch.py**. We have already loaded the YAML. So here, we will now read the threshold:

```
threshold = float(cfg.get("confidence_threshold", 0.70))
print("Confidence threshold:", threshold)
```

The Spark gives us a **probability** column when we run the model. That column contains how strongly the model leans toward each category. We will use the highest value as our confidence score.

So now, we will add the following helper:

```
from pyspark.sql.functions import udf, col
from pyspark.sql.types import DoubleType
def max_prob(v):
    return float(max(v)) if v is not None else 0.0
```

```
max_prob_udf = udf(max_prob, DoubleType())
```

After this, we will include it in our scoring output:

```
tagged_df = pred_df.select(
    "file_path", "sender", "recipients", "sent_at",
    "subject", "body",
    label_udf(col("prediction")).alias("tag"),
    max_prob_udf(col("probability")).alias("confidence")
)
```

Accepted vs. Review Split

Next, we route low-confidence predictions into the review bucket. So here, we will add the following split:

```
from pyspark.sql.functions import lit
scored_df = tagged_df.withColumn(
    "needs_review",
    (col("confidence") < lit(threshold))
)
accepted_df = scored_df.filter(col("needs_review") == False)
review_df   = scored_df.filter(col("needs_review") == True)
```

After this, the system is now saying, "I am not sure about these." That admission is what makes the pipeline safer.

Write Two Outputs

Here, we will keep the accepted results in the normal output locations, and we write review results separately. For this, the following is the accepted one:

```
accepted_df.write.mode("overwrite").parquet(parquet_out)
accepted_df.coalesce(1).write.mode("overwrite").option("header
", "true").csv(csv_out)
```

Now we will write the review outputs:

```
review_parquet_out = cfg["output_review_gold"]
review_csv_out     = cfg["output_review_csv"]
review_df.write.mode("overwrite").parquet(review_parquet_out)
review_df.coalesce(1).write.mode("overwrite").option("header",
"true").csv(review_csv_out)
```

This gives us both the clear streams, one for normal use, and the other for manual checking.

With this, we added a simple safety valve to our private AI pipeline. The job now writes a normal tagged output plus a review bucket for uncertain predictions. The threshold stays in YAML, so changing behavior feels like adjusting a dial, not rewriting logic. Most importantly, our system became more trustworthy because it admitted uncertainty instead of hiding it.

Useful Reporting Layer

The Mailroom Assistant is now handling the tough stuff. It's taking in emails, cleaning them up, tagging them, and even sorting out uncertain cases into a review bucket. Now we've added a practical output layer that feels immediately useful. At its core, a reporting layer is just a set of small tables that handle common questions without needing to read raw email bodies. We want tables that a team lead can glance at and understand what's going on. We want to see how many emails arrived per tag, who sent the most emails, and whether workload is rising or falling week over week.

We'll keep this simple and consistent by treating reports like any other batch job. First, read the Gold table, compute aggregates, and write clean Parquet tables that Spark can query later. Once these tables are set up, dashboards, exports, and audits become a breeze because we're working with summaries instead of raw records.

Let us execute in the following steps:

Using Reporting Job for Tagged Output

To begin with, we create file at **src/mailroom/reporting/daily_report_job.py** and we will design it to read one batch folder from the Gold layer. That way, we can run it for any day and keep the results organized:

```
# daily_report_job.py - block 1
from pyspark.sql import SparkSession
import sys
```

```
spark =
SparkSession.builder.appName("MailroomDailyReports").getOrCrea
te()
run_date = sys.argv[1] if len(sys.argv) > 1 else "2026-02-20"
input_path = f"data/gold/emails_tagged/{run_date}/"
tagged_df = spark.read.parquet(input_path)
print("Rows in tagged batch:", tagged_df.count())
```

This is basically one input, multiple output. If the count is zero, we stop and fix upstream issues, because reports on empty inputs are meaningless.

Tag-wise Daily Counts

The counts by tag are the first table we want. This gives us immediate visibility into what kind of communication dominated the day. We will group by the **tag** column and count rows.

```
# daily_report_job.py - block 2
from pyspark.sql.functions import count
counts_by_tag = tagged_df.groupBy("tag").agg(
    count("*").alias("email_count")
)
```

With this, we write it as a Parquet table. We will keep report tables under **data/reports/** and organize them by date.

```
# daily_report_job.py - block 3
counts_by_tag_out = f"data/reports/counts_by_tag/{run_date}/"
counts_by_tag.write.mode("overwrite").parquet(counts_by_tag_ou
t)
print("Wrote counts_by_tag to:", counts_by_tag_out)
```

This output becomes queryable for Spark, and it also stays small and easy to export later.

Day-wise Top Senders

Here, we will now compute the top senders. This answers a simple question, like ***who generated the most email volume today***? So here, we will group by **sender**, count, and take the top N, like Ten is a very good start to me.

```python
# daily_report_job.py - block 4
from pyspark.sql.functions import desc
top_senders = tagged_df.groupBy("sender").agg(
    count("*").alias("email_count")
).orderBy(desc("email_count")).limit(10)
```

Now write it:

```python
# daily_report_job.py - block 5
top_senders_out = f"data/reports/top_senders/{run_date}/"
top_senders.write.mode("overwrite").parquet(top_senders_out)
print("Wrote top_senders to:", top_senders_out)
```

This table is also valuable for triage. If one sender spikes dramatically, it often points to an incident, an automated system, or a policy update being circulated.

Weekly Trend Lines

After this, we now want the trend lines, and that too by week. And, this is where the system begins to show patterns like, ***is Ops traffic rising?, is Legal volume spiking?,*** or ***is HR steady***?

So here, we will take the **`sent_at`** timestamp and derive a week bucket. The Spark can do this neatly with **`date_trunc`** or **`weekofyear`**. We will use **`date_trunc("week", ...)`** because it produces a stable week start date.

```python
# daily_report_job.py - block 6
from pyspark.sql.functions import date_trunc, col
weekly_df = tagged_df.withColumn(
    "week_start",
    date_trunc("week", col("sent_at"))
)
```

Next, we aggregate counts by **`week_start`** and **`tag`**.

```python
# daily_report_job.py - block 7
weekly_trends = weekly_df.groupBy("week_start", "tag").agg(
    count("*").alias("email_count")
```

```
).orderBy("week_start", "tag")
```

Now write it as shown below:

```
# daily_report_job.py - block 8
weekly_trends_out =
f"data/reports/weekly_trends_by_tag/{run_date}/"
weekly_trends.write.mode("overwrite").parquet(weekly_trends_ou
t)
print("Wrote weekly trends to:", weekly_trends_out)
```

This weekly table will later support charts, comparisons, and summaries. Because it is Parquet, the Spark can filter, group, and join it instantly.

Running Reporting Job

After all this, we now run the job for a given date:

```
spark-submit src/mailroom/reporting/daily_report_job.py 2026-
02-20
```

And, we can run it for any day as long as the corresponding date exists.

Querying Report Tables

And there is another important thing which is the benefit of storing reports as Parquet tables. In a Spark shell or a small script, we can do it by the following script:

```
counts = spark.read.parquet("data/reports/counts_by_tag/2026-
02-20/")
counts.show()
weekly =
spark.read.parquet("data/reports/weekly_trends_by_tag/2026-02-
20/")
weekly.filter(weekly.tag ==
"Ops").orderBy("week_start").show()
```

This gives us a reporting layer that feels simple, stays queryable, and gives immediate value. This reporting layer keeps our private AI system usable for teams, because it turns raw predictions into small, structured summaries that support everyday decisions.

Error Handling and Retry Strategy

One messy email shouldn't stop the whole batch when we run batch scoring in the real world. There's a chance a single record could be malformed, missing fields, or contain content that breaks one of our small helper functions. If our job fails hard, we lose time, we lose trust, and we end up rerunning the same batch again and again without learning what actually went wrong.

So, we're going to add two simple habits. First, we're going to capture errors in a structured way at the record level so the batch keeps moving. Second, we're going to store those failed records in a quarantine table so we can inspect them later, fix the root causes, and reprocess only what failed. We're keeping this topic on the practical side. We're not going to build a heavy framework. We'll add a few columns, split them into "good" and "quarantine" sets, and write both as Parquet so Spark can query them whenever it needs to.

Add Validation Columns

To begin with, we will first return to **src/mailroom/ml/score_batch.py**. And, right after we read **emails_df** from the Silver batch, we will add the validation columns. We will keep this logic readable by using **when** expressions rather than tricky code.

```
# score_batch.py - validation block
from pyspark.sql.functions import col, when, lit, length
validated_df = emails_df.withColumn(
    "error_reason",
    when(col("file_path").isNull() | (col("file_path") == ""),
lit("missing_file_path"))
    .when((col("subject").isNull() | (col("subject") == "")) &
(col("body").isNull() | (col("body") == "")),
lit("empty_subject_and_body"))
    .when(col("sent_at").isNull(), lit("missing_sent_at"))
    .otherwise(lit(None))
).withColumn(
    "is_valid",
    col("error_reason").isNull()
)
```

With this, we split early. The valid rows go to scoring and the invalid rows go straight to quarantine. This keeps the model stage clean and avoids confusing outcomes.

```
# score_batch.py - split block
good_input_df = validated_df.filter(col("is_valid") ==
True).drop("is_valid")
bad_input_df  = validated_df.filter(col("is_valid") == False)
```

Scoring and Scoring Errors

The Spark ML transform usually does not fail per record, but the helper UDFs can. However, we avoid that risk by making our helpers defensive. We already used safe functions in the earlier topic, and we will keep them safe by returning defaults when values are missing.

```
# score_batch.py - safe helpers block
from pyspark.sql.functions import udf
from pyspark.sql.types import StringType, DoubleType
labels = model.stages[0].labels
def id_to_label_safe(i):
    try:
        j = int(i)
        return labels[j] if 0 <= j < len(labels) else
"unknown"
    except Exception:
        return "unknown"
def max_prob_safe(v):
    try:
        return float(max(v)) if v is not None else 0.0
    except Exception:
        return 0.0
label_udf = udf(id_to_label_safe, StringType())
max_prob_udf = udf(max_prob_safe, DoubleType())
```

With this, we score only the good inputs. After scoring, we can also guard against unexpected missing **`probability`** values by routing those rows into quarantine as well as sohwn below:

```
# score_batch.py - scoring block
```

```
pred_df = model.transform(good_input_df)
scored_df = pred_df.select(
    "file_path", "sender", "recipients", "sent_at",
    "subject", "body",
    label_udf(col("prediction")).alias("tag"),
    max_prob_udf(col("probability")).alias("confidence")
)
scored_with_checks = scored_df.withColumn(
    "error_reason",
    when(col("confidence").isNull(),
lit("missing_confidence"))
    .otherwise(lit(None))
).withColumn(
    "is_valid",
    col("error_reason").isNull()
)
good_scored_df = scored_with_checks.filter(col("is_valid") ==
True).drop("is_valid", "error_reason")
bad_scored_df  = scored_with_checks.filter(col("is_valid") ==
False)
```

Quarantine Table for Spark Query

Now here, we will try to unify the quarantine from both, pre-scoring invalid rows and post-scoring invalid rows. Here, we will also add a few useful columns so quarantined records tell us what happened, when, and in which run, as shown below:

```
# score_batch.py - quarantine block
from pyspark.sql.functions import current_timestamp
quarantine_df = bad_input_df.select(
    "file_path", "sender", "recipients", "sent_at", "subject",
"body", "error_reason"
).unionByName(
```

```
    bad_scored_df.select("file_path", "sender", "recipients", 
"sent_at", "subject", "body", "error_reason")
).withColumn(
    "stage", lit("batch_scoring")
).withColumn(
    "run_date", lit(run_date)
).withColumn(
    "model_dir", lit(model_path)
).withColumn(
    "quarantined_at", current_timestamp()
)
quarantine_out = "data/quarantine/emails/"
quarantine_df.write.mode("append").parquet(quarantine_out)
print("Quarantine rows written:", quarantine_df.count())
```

This table is now queryable forever. If someone asks why an email did not appear in the report, we can point to a row in quarantine with a clear reason.

Retry Helper

Some failures are transient, especially on shared storage. So here, we will use the retry logic. We will wrap the writes in a helper that retries a few times before failing the job. This does not hide real problems, but it prevents one temporary hiccup from wasting a full rerun.

```
# score_batch.py - retry helper block
import time
def write_parquet_with_retry(df, path, mode="overwrite", 
retries=3, pause_seconds=3):
    attempt = 1
    while attempt <= retries:
        try:
            df.write.mode(mode).parquet(path)
            return
        except Exception as e:
```

```
            print(f"Write failed (attempt
{attempt}/{retries}): {e}")
            if attempt == retries:
                raise
            time.sleep(pause_seconds)
            attempt += 1
```

And after this, we use them for our main output tables:

```
# score_batch.py - write outputs with retry
write_parquet_with_retry(good_scored_df, parquet_out,
mode="overwrite")
```

Once quarantine exists, we can use it in a calm and repeatable way. We can query it by run date, count how many failures happened, and see the top reasons. That information often points directly to the next improvement, such as tightening earlier parsing, improving cleaning rules, or expanding label coverage. When we are ready to reprocess, we do not rerun the full batch. We filter quarantine rows, fix the issue, and run them through scoring again. This is how private AI stays reliable without pretending that data is always perfect.

Summary

To sum up, we turned the trained tagger into a dependable batch component that processed new email snapshots without changing code each time. We used a small YAML file to pin the input batch, the exact model version, and the output locations, then built a scoring job that loaded the saved Spark pipeline and produced a clean Gold table. The job wrote results as Parquet for downstream Spark work and also exported a CSV for quick sharing outside Spark. We then added a simple confidence score and a configurable threshold so uncertain predictions were routed into a separate "needs review" bucket, which made the system safer by admitting uncertainty instead of hiding it.

Later, we then added a lightweight reporting layer that produced daily aggregates such as counts by tag, top senders, and weekly trend lines, and we stored each output as its own Parquet table so Spark could query them easily later. Finally, we introduced structured error capture that kept batch processing moving even when individual records were problematic. We marked invalid inputs with clear error reasons and wrote failed items into a quarantine table with run details, making failures searchable and actionable rather than silent. With these patterns in place, our batch pipeline stayed practical, repeatable, and auditable while producing outputs that teams could use immediately.

CHAPTER 5: SMART SUMMARIES

Overview

In this chapter we will add summaries in a careful, beginner-friendly way that keeps our private workflow honest. We will start with a baseline approach that does not require any LLM, where we will split each email into sentences, score those sentences using keyword overlap from our existing keywords column, and assemble a short extractive summary that reuses only sentences already present in the message. We will store this result as baseline_summary in a queryable Gold table so our reporting and downstream exports can use summaries without touching full email bodies, and we will keep the implementation in small code blocks that we can follow line by line.

After the baseline exists, we will put quality gates around it so summary output stays dependable across future batches. We will enforce simple checks such as a maximum length rule, banned pattern detection for obvious forwarded markers and disclaimer lines, and a strict empty-output check so failures become visible instead of silent. We will route failures into a quarantine table with clear reasons, record per-run QC counts as small tables, and generate a small sampled set for human review that fits naturally into our workflow. We will then prepare for optional future LLM usage by chunking long emails into predictable pieces with a maximum size and a small overlap, storing prompt templates as files, and recording a prompt version fingerprint so every prepared request remains traceable to the exact wording and chunking settings that produced it.

Summaries without LLM

We will noe begin. To start with, we will first add summaries to our Mailroom Assistant, but we will do it carefully. We will not use any LLM yet. We will build a baseline that stays safe, predictable, and easy to debug. Our baseline summary will be extractive, which means it will only pick sentences that already exist in the email body. That alone reduces risk because the system does not invent anything. We will rank sentences using two signals we already trust: keyword overlap and a simple sentence ranking rule. Then we will store the result as a new column named **`baseline_summary`** so downstream jobs can query it like any other table.

Create Summarization Job Skeleton

We will begin to create a file at **`src/mailroom/nlp/summary_baseline_job.py`** along with a Spark session and two paths (one input and one output). We will follow the same "**`run_date`**" pattern we used in batch scoring and reporting, because it keeps our pipeline consistent.

```
# summary_baseline_job.py - block 1
from pyspark.sql import SparkSession
import sys
```

```
spark =
SparkSession.builder.appName("BaselineSummaries").getOrCreate(
)
run_date = sys.argv[1] if len(sys.argv) > 1 else "2026-02-20"
input_path = f"data/gold/emails_keywords/{run_date}/"
output_path = f"data/gold/emails_summaries/{run_date}/"
df = spark.read.parquet(input_path)
print("Rows loaded:", df.count())
```

This block confirms we are reading the batch we expect. If the count is zero, we pause and correct the upstream keyword output path for that run date.

Split Email Body into Sentences

Next, we will now create a small helper that splits the email body into sentences. We keep it simple: normalize whitespace, then split on punctuation boundaries. This will never be perfect, but it will be stable, and that is what we want for a baseline.

```
# summary_baseline_job.py - block 2
import re
def split_sentences(text):
    if text is None:
        return []
    cleaned = re.sub(r"\s+", " ", text).strip()
    if cleaned == "":
        return []
    parts = re.split(r"(?<=[.!?])\s+", cleaned)
    return [p.strip() for p in parts if p.strip()]
```

This function does one job and does it in a calm way. We now have the building block needed for ranking.

Sentence Scoring using Keyword Overlap

This is quite important now. Here, we will now decide which sentences matter most. If a sentence contains more of the extracted keywords, it is more likely to be important. We will also add a gentle length bonus so extremely tiny sentences do not dominate just because they contain one keyword.

```
# summary_baseline_job.py - block 3
def score_sentence(sentence, keywords_set):
    s = sentence.lower()
    hits = 0
    for k in keywords_set:
        if k and k.lower() in s:
            hits += 1
    length_bonus = min(len(sentence) / 200.0, 1.0)
    return (hits * 2.0) + length_bonus
```

This scoring rule stays explainable: more keyword matches means higher rank, and medium-length sentences get a small boost because they often carry more context.

Build Extractive Baseline Summary

Now we stitch the previous helpers into one function that returns the summary text. We will pick the top three sentences. After selecting, we keep original order so the result reads naturally. We will also avoid extremely short sentences and repeated lines.

```
# summary_baseline_job.py - block 4
def build_baseline_summary(subject, body, keywords,
max_sentences=3):
    keys = set([k for k in (keywords or []) if k])
    sentences = split_sentences(body)
    usable = [s for s in sentences if len(s) >= 30]
    if len(usable) == 0:
        return subject if subject else ""
    scored = []
    for i, s in enumerate(usable):
        scored.append((i, s, score_sentence(s, keys)))
    scored.sort(key=lambda x: x[2], reverse=True)
    chosen = scored[:max_sentences]
```

```
    chosen.sort(key=lambda x: x[0])
    seen = set()
    final = []
    for _, s, _ in chosen:
        if s not in seen:
            final.append(s)
            seen.add(s)
    return " ".join(final).strip()
```

This is the entire baseline idea in one place. No external services, no heavy libraries, and the output stays grounded in the original email.

Apply Summary Function

We will now create a UDF and store the output, for every row in a new column named **`baseline_summary`**. This is the column we will carry forward in later topics.

```
# summary_baseline_job.py - block 5
from pyspark.sql.functions import udf, col
from pyspark.sql.types import StringType
summary_udf = udf(build_baseline_summary, StringType())
out_df = df.withColumn(
    "baseline_summary",
    summary_udf(col("subject"), col("body"), col("keywords"))
)
```

At this point we have summaries. Now we decide what to store in the output table.

Write Clean Gold Table with Baseline Summaries

We will include tag and keywords so downstream reporting can use them without joining multiple tables. And, we need to keep the body out of the summary table to reduce size, because we already have bodies stored elsewhere.

```
# summary_baseline_job.py - block 6
final_df = out_df.select(
```

```
    "file_path", "sender", "recipients", "sent_at",
    "subject", "tag", "keywords",
    "baseline_summary"
)
final_df.write.mode("overwrite").parquet(output_path)
print("Wrote summaries to:", output_path)
```

After this, the Spark can query summaries instantly, and our reporting layer can consume this table without touching raw email bodies.

And finally, we run it like the rest of our batch jobs:

```
spark-submit src/mailroom/nlp/summary_baseline_job.py 2026-02-20
```

At the end, we have a queryable table at:

```
data/gold/emails_summaries/2026-02-20/
```

With this, we created a baseline summarization job that stayed safe and beginner-friendly. We split emails into sentences, ranked sentences using keyword overlap and simple rules, stitched the best sentences into an extractive summary, and stored it as **`baseline_summary`** in a Gold table. The code stayed understandable because we built it in small blocks, each doing one clear job, and we ended with a quick check that told us if the output looked healthy.

Summary Quality Checks

Our baseline summaries now exist as a **`baseline_summary`** column in the Gold layer, and that is a big step forward. A summary column also introduces silent degradation which is a rick to us. A small change in parsing, cleaning, or keyword extraction can quietly produce summaries that are empty, too long, or filled with noisy boilerplate. So here too, we need to add quality gates that run every time, and we will store the results as tables so we can track behavior across runs.

Our goal in this topic is to develop a calm workflow where we catch obvious issues early, quarantine bad outputs, and pull a small sample for human review so we stay grounded in what the system is actually producing.

Config for Summary Quality Gates

To start with, we will try to keep the rules adjustable, which are without the code edits. And for this, we will create **`configs/summary_quality.yaml`** which will define a maximum summary length, a few banned patterns we do not want in summaries, and the size of our human review sample, as shown below:

```
run_date: "2026-02-20"
max_chars: 600
banned_patterns:
  - "(?i)forwarded by"
  - "(?i)original message"
  - "(?i)confidentiality notice"
  - "(?i)please consider the environment"
sample_size: 30
sample_seed: 42
```

Now, this YAML file will tell a simple story, like the summaries should stay short, we need to avoid a small set of noisy markers, and we have to always produce a small review set. We can tune these values later when we see real outputs, but the job will stay stable.

Summary Read Quality Check

For this, we will create **src/mailroom/nlp/summary_quality_job.py** which will read the batch summary table and keep our code in small blocks. We will also load the YAML first so the job always reflects the configured policy.

```
# summary_quality_job.py - block 1
from pyspark.sql import SparkSession
import yaml
spark =
SparkSession.builder.appName("SummaryQualityChecks").getOrCrea
te()
with open("configs/summary_quality.yaml") as f:
    cfg = yaml.safe_load(f)
run_date = cfg["run_date"]
max_chars = int(cfg["max_chars"])
banned_patterns = cfg["banned_patterns"]
sample_size = int(cfg["sample_size"])
```

```
sample_seed = int(cfg["sample_seed"])
input_path = f"data/gold/emails_summaries/{run_date}/"
df = spark.read.parquet(input_path)
print("Rows loaded for QC:", df.count())
```

This job expects that **baseline_summary** already exists. If rows load correctly, we move to checks. If rows do not load, we fix the upstream summarization job for that date before any further work.

Simple Checks

We will add three checks that catch the most common issues. First, we will reject empty summaries. Second, we will reject summaries above a maximum length. Third, we will reject summaries that match any banned pattern.

And, we will store failures with clear reasons, because such clarity helps us decide what to fix later.

```
# summary_quality_job.py - block 2
from pyspark.sql.functions import col, length, lit, when
qc_df = df.withColumn(
    "qc_reason",
    when(col("baseline_summary").isNull() |
(col("baseline_summary") == ""), lit("empty_summary"))
    .when(length(col("baseline_summary")) > lit(max_chars),
lit("summary_too_long"))
    .otherwise(lit(None))
)
```

After this, we will then add banned pattern checks. We will keep the logic easy to read by creating one boolean column per pattern, then collapsing into a single reason. The Spark can evaluate these checks at scale, and it will keep it efficient because it stays column based.

```
# summary_quality_job.py - block 3
from pyspark.sql.functions import expr
pattern_checks = []
for i, pat in enumerate(banned_patterns):
```

```
    pattern_checks.append(expr(f"baseline_summary rlike
'{pat}'").alias(f"ban_{i}"))
flags_df = qc_df.select("*", *pattern_checks)
```

After this, we convert the pattern flags into a single reason when no earlier reason exists:

```
# summary_quality_job.py - block 4
from pyspark.sql.functions import greatest
ban_cols = [col(f"ban_{i}").cast("int") for i in
range(len(banned_patterns))]
flags_sum = None
for c in ban_cols:
    flags_sum = c if flags_sum is None else (flags_sum + c)
qc_df2 = flags_df.withColumn(
    "qc_reason",
    when(col("qc_reason").isNotNull(), col("qc_reason"))
    .when(flags_sum > lit(0), lit("banned_pattern"))
    .otherwise(lit(None))
).withColumn(
    "qc_pass",
    col("qc_reason").isNull()
)
```

This gives each row a clear outcome, like **qc_pass** holds either true or false, and **qc_reason** holds a single reason for failures.

Write Failed Summaries into Quarantine Table

We will not drop failures. We will quarantine them. This table will allow later inspection, counts by reason, and focused reprocessing. We will store enough context to understand what happened without pulling the full email body.

```
# summary_quality_job.py - block 5
from pyspark.sql.functions import current_timestamp
quarantine_df = qc_df2.filter(col("qc_pass") == False).select(
```

```
    "file_path", "sent_at", "tag", "keywords",
"baseline_summary", "qc_reason"
).withColumn(
    "run_date", lit(run_date)
).withColumn(
    "quarantined_at", current_timestamp()
)
quarantine_out = "data/quarantine/summaries/"
quarantine_df.write.mode("append").parquet(quarantine_out)
print("Quarantined summaries:", quarantine_df.count())
```

Next, we then write the passing set back out as a "checked" table. It keeps downstream jobs clean because they can use the checked table as their source of truth.

```
# summary_quality_job.py - block 6
passed_df = qc_df2.filter(col("qc_pass") == True).drop(
    *[f"ban_{i}" for i in range(len(banned_patterns))]
)
passed_out = f"data/gold/emails_summaries_checked/{run_date}/"
passed_df.write.mode("overwrite").parquet(passed_out)
print("Checked summaries written:", passed_out)
```

Store QC Metrics

We will store simple counts so we can see trends over time. We will compute totals, pass count, fail count, and failure reasons. We will write them as a small Parquet table for this run date.

```
# summary_quality_job.py - block 7
from pyspark.sql.functions import count
summary_counts =
qc_df2.groupBy("qc_pass").agg(count("*").alias("rows"))
reason_counts = qc_df2.filter(col("qc_pass") ==
False).groupBy("qc_reason").agg(count("*").alias("rows"))
```

```
summary_counts_out =
f"data/reports/summary_qc_counts/{run_date}/"

reason_counts_out =
f"data/reports/summary_qc_reasons/{run_date}/"

summary_counts.write.mode("overwrite").parquet(summary_counts_
out)

reason_counts.write.mode("overwrite").parquet(reason_counts_ou
t)

print("QC metrics written for run_date:", run_date)
```

These two tiny tables become our early warning system. A rising count of **`empty_summary`** or **`banned_pattern`** tells us something upstream changed.

And lastly, we run the QC job just like our other batch steps:

```
spark-submit src/mailroom/nlp/summary_quality_job.py
```

With this, we've successfully set up a quality gate in our pipeline. It keeps bad summaries out, stores metrics, and puts together a small review pack for humans. Overall, it keep things from getting worse over time and makes sure the summary is consistently done well, not just once.

Data Preparation for LLM Calls

We have intentionally stayed away from LLM calls so far, and that discipline has served us well. Still, teams often reach a point where they want to try a private LLM step for selected tasks, such as richer summaries or structured extraction. The risky part is not the model call itself, rather the long emails that do not fit cleanly, the prompts that quietly change over time, and the outputs that later become impossible to explain.

This topic sets up the safety rails before any model call exists. We will prepare email content into small, predictable chunks, we will store prompt templates as files so edits stay visible, and we will record prompt versions so every prepared request remains traceable. Once we have this preparation layer, we can treat future LLM usage as a controlled plug-in rather than a messy ad-hoc step.

Chunking Rules and Prompt Templates

The concept of chunking rules describes how we split a long email into smaller pieces that still make sense on their own. So here, our rules will be simple and configurable, wherein we will build chunks up to a maximum size, we will keep a small overlap between chunks to preserve context, and we will avoid tiny chunks that usually contain only signatures.

And, the prompt templates are plain text files that hold the instruction we would send to a model. We will not hard-code prompts inside Python because prompt wording is part of system behavior. When prompts live as files, we can review them, version them, and compare changes over time. Finally, we will compute a prompt version fingerprint from the template content and the chunking settings, then write that version into our run logs. This gives us the ability to answer a critical question later: which prompt template and which chunking rules produced these prepared requests.

Add Config file

To start with, we will first create **configs/llm_prep.yaml**:

```
run_date: "2026-02-20"
input_path:  "data/gold/emails_tagged/2026-02-20/"
output_path: "data/gold/llm_prep/2026-02-20/"
chunking:
  max_chars: 2200
  overlap_chars: 200
  min_chunk_chars: 400
prompt:
  name: "email_summary_v1"
  template_path: "prompts/summary_v1.txt"
```

This file keeps our behavior adjustable without touching code.

Store Prompt Template

Next, we will then create **prompts/summary_v1.txt**. This template is just a file. Our preparation step will fill the placeholders mentioned in the below script.

```
TASK: Write a short, factual summary of the email chunk.
RULES:
- Use only information present in the chunk.
- Keep it under 4 sentences.
- If the chunk is only a signature or disclaimer, return an
empty string.
CONTEXT:
```

```
Subject: {subject}
From: {sender}
Date: {sent_at}
Chunk {chunk_id} of {chunk_total}
EMAIL CHUNK:
{chunk_text}
```

Chunking and Prompt Handling

Next, we will then create **src/mailroom/nlp/chunking.py** for chunking.

```
import re
def split_sentences(text: str) -> list[str]:
    if not text:
        return []
    cleaned = re.sub(r"\s+", " ", text).strip()
    if not cleaned:
        return []
    parts = re.split(r"(?<=[.!?])\s+", cleaned)
    return [p.strip() for p in parts if p.strip()]
def make_chunks(text: str, max_chars: int, overlap_chars: int,
min_chunk_chars: int) -> list[str]:
    sentences = split_sentences(text)
    if not sentences:
        return []
    chunks, current = [], ""
    for s in sentences:
        if len(current) + len(s) + 1 <= max_chars:
            current = (current + " " + s).strip()
        else:
            if len(current) >= min_chunk_chars:
```

```
                chunks.append(current)
            current = s
    if len(current) >= min_chunk_chars:
        chunks.append(current)
    if overlap_chars > 0 and len(chunks) > 1:
        chunks = [chunks[0]] + [(chunks[i-1][-overlap_chars:]
+ " " + chunks[i]).strip() for i in range(1, len(chunks))]
    return chunks
```

After this, we will then put the prompt handling and versioning into another helper. And for this, we will create **src/mailroom/nlp/prompting.py**:

```
import hashlib
import json
def read_template(path: str) -> str:
    with open(path, "r", encoding="utf-8") as f:
        return f.read()
def sha256_text(text: str) -> str:
    return hashlib.sha256(text.encode("utf-8")).hexdigest()
def compute_prompt_version(template_text: str, chunk_cfg:
dict, prompt_name: str) -> str:
    payload = {
        "prompt_name": prompt_name,
        "template_sha": sha256_text(template_text),
        "chunking": chunk_cfg
    }
    return sha256_text(json.dumps(payload, sort_keys=True))
def render_prompt(template_text: str, subject: str, sender:
str, sent_at: str,
                  chunk_id: int, chunk_total: int, chunk_text:
str) -> str:
    return template_text.format(
```

```
        subject=subject or "",
        sender=sender or "",
        sent_at=sent_at or "",
        chunk_id=chunk_id,
        chunk_total=chunk_total,
        chunk_text=chunk_text
    )
```

This stage is pretty straightforward. We just do the basics like, read emails, chunk bodies, render prompts, write a Parquet table, and write a one-row log containing the prompt version. We can use the same small-block approach we used earlier, with these helpers so no single block becomes hard to follow.

Summary

Basically, we added summaries, but we started with a baseline that was safe and local. We made these summaries by taking each email and breaking it into sentences. Then, we used the keywords from our keywords column and a simple scoring rule to rank those sentences. And then, we put the top sentences back together in the order they were originally written. We then treated summary quality as a routine habit that protected us from silent degradation.

We put clear gates in place, like a maximum length limit, and we banned pattern checks for obvious forwarded markers and disclaimer noise. We also had strict empty-output detection. We put the failures into a quarantine table with one reason for each record, and we wrote small metrics tables so we could track pass rates and failure reasons across runs. We also put together a small sample set for human review, mixing mostly passing items with a few quarantined items, which kept our judgment grounded in real outputs. At last, we got ready for possible future LLM use by setting up rules for chunking, saving prompt templates as files, and recording a prompt version fingerprint for tracking.

CHAPTER 6: BOOSTING WITH vLLM INTEGRATION

Overview

In this chapter we will explore how an optional acceleration layer can fit into our private AI architecture without disrupting the discipline we have built so far. We will introduce vLLM as an internal inference service and clearly define how it complements Spark rather than competing with it. You will learn how to evaluate local LLM models based on hardware constraints and licensing requirements, document your selection decision, and store model weights inside your controlled offline assets structure. The emphasis will remain on engineering fit and reproducibility rather than on chasing larger models or abstract performance claims.

As the chapter progresses, you will implement a Spark-to-vLLM batch integration module that sends prepared prompts per partition, captures responses, and records structured trace metadata. You will see how to isolate failures into quarantine tables so the batch continues safely. Finally, you will measure performance using simple but meaningful metrics such as latency and throughput, compare different inference approaches for the same summarization workload, and store those measurements per run for future comparison. By the end of the chapter, you will understand how acceleration can be introduced carefully, observed objectively, and integrated without compromising traceability or control.

Where vLLM fits in our architecture

We already have a clean mental model for private AI: Apache Spark prepares and enriches data in batch, then writes queryable tables that the rest of our workflow can trust. Now we add one optional acceleration component, and we keep the boundary sharp. vLLM is not a data engine, and Spark is not a low-latency model server. vLLM exists to run large language models efficiently as a service, focusing on high throughput and predictable GPU memory behavior through techniques like continuous batching and PagedAttention.

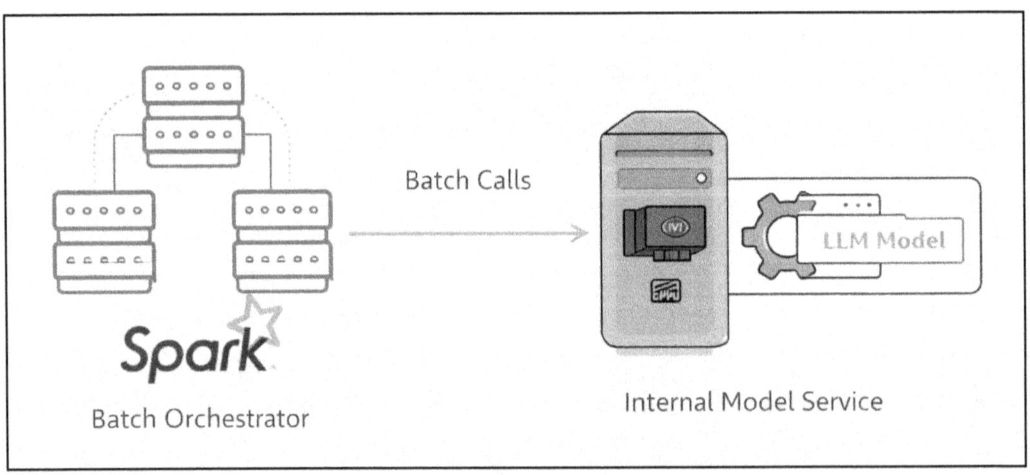

Fig 6.1 LLMs in Architecture

The Spark exists to handle large-scale transforms, batching, scheduling, and storage. When we combine them, the Spark becomes the batch orchestrator that feeds prepared chunks to vLLM, while vLLM becomes the internal inference engine that returns model outputs. This division keeps our system honest, wherein the Spark stays in charge of data, versions, and tables, and vLLM stays in charge of fast inference on dedicated hardware.

Saprk vs. vLLM

The Spark gives us the benefit of repeatability, lineage, and bulk data movement. We used it to tag emails, create review buckets, generate reports, and store logs as Parquet. Those outputs remain valuable even if we never call a model server.

Whereas, the vLLM gives us an internal endpoint that behaves like a component. It can expose an OpenAI-compatible HTTP interface, which means our batch job can call it with standard request shapes and treat it like a private service.

	Apache Spark	vLLM
Primary Role:	Data Processing & Batch Orchestration	LLM Inference Serving
Data Handling:	Large-Scale Data Transformations	Fast Model Execution on GPUs
Request Type:	Pulls Processed Data in Batches	Serves Requests Continuously
Interface:	Reads/Writes Tables & Files	OpenAI-Compatible API
Failure Handling:	Retry & Quarantine Failed Jobs	Handle Transient Errors

Fig 6.2 Spark vs. vLLM Contribution to Private AI

The key difference is that the Spark "pulls" work in big partitions, while vLLM "serves" model work continuously, batching requests internally for higher throughput. In our architecture, the Spark owns chunk creation, prompt versioning, and per-record traceability. vLLM owns model loading, GPU scheduling, and request execution. This keeps failure handling straightforward because the Spark can quarantine failed calls and continue, while vLLM can focus on inference rather than storage or long-running ETL.

Running vLLM as Internal Service

We will treat vLLM like any other internal service, like one host, one port, one health expectation, and a clear contract for request and response. The vLLM provides an OpenAI-compatible server that we can start with the **vllm serve** command. We will keep it private by binding it to an internal interface, setting an API key, and placing it behind our internal network controls. The service should run close to GPUs, while the Spark can run on CPU-heavy nodes and call the service over the network in batch.

We will also keep a small operational rule, that the vLLM service should start, load the model, and remain stable across batch windows, rather than starting and stopping for every Spark job.

Start the service (one command, one endpoint):

```
vllm serve NousResearch/Meta-Llama-3-8B-Instruct --host
0.0.0.0 --port 8000 --api-key token-abc123
```

This command uses the OpenAI-compatible frontend and exposes the server on port 8000. In our private environment, we typically bind to a private IP rather than **0.0.0.0**, but the structure stays the same. We now have a single internal base URL, for example **http://vllm-internal:8000**. From this point onward, the Spark does not "know" anything about GPUs. The Spark only knows it can post JSON requests to an internal endpoint and receive JSON responses.

Spark Calling vLLM in Batch

We'll just assume we've already got the chunk rows and prompt text ready in our **llm_prep** table from the last topic. That table is our bridge: one row equals one request unit. Now, we're going to set up a small batch caller in Spark that reads a limited batch, calls vLLM, and writes the results to a Parquet table and a quarantine table for failures.

So here, we'll first break the code into short blocks so we can follow it without getting lost.

```
from pyspark.sql import SparkSession

spark =
SparkSession.builder.appName("LLMBatchCalls").getOrCreate()

run_date = "2026-02-20"

prep_path = f"data/gold/llm_prep/{run_date}/"

df = spark.read.parquet(prep_path)

work_df = df.select("file_path", "chunk_id", "chunk_total",
"prompt_text", "prompt_version")

print("Prepared rows:", work_df.count())
```

After this, since the vLLM serves an OpenAI-compatible API, so we call the chat completions endpoint using a standard JSON shape.

```
import time
import requests
BASE_URL = "http://vllm-internal:8000"
API_KEY = "token-abc123"
def call_vllm_chat(prompt_text, timeout_s=60):
    headers = {"Authorization": f"Bearer {API_KEY}"}
    payload = {
        "model": "NousResearch/Meta-Llama-3-8B-Instruct",
        "messages": [{"role": "user", "content":
prompt_text}],
        "temperature": 0.0
    }
    t0 = time.time()
    r = requests.post(f"{BASE_URL}/v1/chat/completions",
json=payload, headers=headers, timeout=timeout_s)
    latency_ms = int((time.time() - t0) * 1000)
    return r.status_code, r.text, latency_ms
```

Next, we have to process in partitions. Each partition will call vLLM sequentially, which keeps logic simple. Later, if we need higher throughput, we can increase concurrency per partition, but we will start with clarity.

```
from pyspark.sql.types import StructType, StructField,
StringType, IntegerType, LongType
out_schema = StructType([
    StructField("file_path", StringType(), True),
    StructField("chunk_id", IntegerType(), True),
    StructField("prompt_version", StringType(), True),
    StructField("status_code", IntegerType(), True),
    StructField("latency_ms", LongType(), True),
    StructField("response_text", StringType(), True),
    StructField("error_type", StringType(), True),
```

```
])
def classify_error(status_code, body):
    if status_code == 200:
        return None
    if status_code in (408, 429, 500, 502, 503, 504):
        return "retryable_http"
    return "non_retryable_http"
def run_partition(rows):
    for row in rows:
        try:
            status, body, latency =
call_vllm_chat(row.prompt_text)
            err = classify_error(status, body)
            yield (row.file_path, int(row.chunk_id),
row.prompt_version, int(status), int(latency), body, err)
        except Exception:
            yield (row.file_path, int(row.chunk_id),
row.prompt_version, 0, 0, "", "network_or_timeout")
rdd = work_df.rdd.mapPartitions(run_partition)
results_df = spark.createDataFrame(rdd, schema=out_schema)
```

After this, we will then write the results and quarantine tables:

```
ok_df = results_df.filter(results_df.status_code == 200)
bad_df = results_df.filter(results_df.status_code != 200)
ok_out = f"data/gold/llm_results/{run_date}/"
bad_out = "data/quarantine/llm_calls/"
ok_df.write.mode("overwrite").parquet(ok_out)
bad_df.write.mode("append").parquet(bad_out)
print("OK rows:", ok_df.count())
print("Quarantine rows:", bad_df.count())
```

This keeps our batch moving and gives us a structured quarantine table that Spark can query later, exactly like our earlier patterns.

Documenting Request Flow and Failure Behavior

The next step is to capture the system behavior in one small repo document, because future us will want a single place to understand the flow.

So for this, we will create **`docs/vllm_request_flow.md`** with a short, concrete sequence as shown below:

1. The Spark reads **`data/gold/llm_prep/<run_date>/`** rows.
2. The Spark then sends each **`prompt_text`** to **`http://vllm-internal:8000/v1/chat/completions`**.
3. After this, the vLLM batches requests internally and returns JSON responses.
4. Next, the Spark writes successes to **`data/gold/llm_results/<run_date>/`**.
5. Finally, the Spark writes failures to **`data/quarantine/llm_calls/`** with **`status_code`**, **`latency_ms`**, and **`prompt_version`**.

For failure behavior, we keep it simple and explicit. HTTP timeouts and transient server errors are retryable, while malformed requests and persistent client errors are not. vLLM can also hit GPU memory limits or queue pressure depending on model size and server settings, so our Spark job treats these as retryable infrastructure failures and moves the record to quarantine after the retry policy is exhausted.

Hardware-friendly Local LLM

Until now, we treated the vLLM as a black box that runs a model efficiently. Now we step one layer deeper. The model itself is an engineering constraint. It is not just a capability decision. It is a hardware decision, a memory decision, a licensing decision, and sometimes a legal decision.

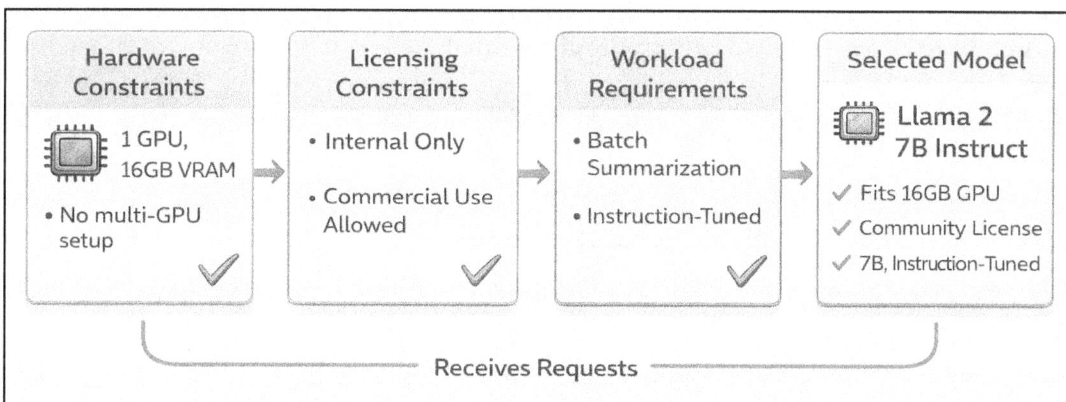

Fig 6.3 LLM Constraints

If we choose a model that does not fit our GPU memory, the system fails at startup. If we choose a model with unclear licensing, we risk compliance issues. If we choose a model that is too large for our workload, we waste resources.

Local LLM MarketPlace

The most practical platform for browsing open-weight large language models is ***Hugging Face***. It hosts thousands of models with metadata including size, architecture, license, and usage instructions. Another common source is TheBloke repositories, which provide quantized versions of popular models.

For this topic, we will keep the workflow straightforward and browse the model page on Hugging Face. When evaluating a candidate model, we look at four fields:

1. Parameter size such as 7B or 13B
2. Required GPU memory in full precision and quantized modes
3. License type such as Apache 2.0 or custom community license
4. Intended usage such as chat or instruction tuning

Here, we are not optimizing for raw capability. We are just trying to optimize for feasibility within our infrastructure.

Translating Hardware into Model Constraints

Before choosing a model, we must state our hardware clearly. Our current environment includes:

- One GPU with 16 GB VRAM
- 64 GB system RAM
- No multi-GPU setup

So here, a 7B parameter model in 16-bit precision can require around 14 to 16 GB VRAM depending on implementation. A quantized 4-bit version can reduce this substantially. And, the larger models such as 13B may exceed safe limits unless heavily quantized.

Therefore, for our 16 GB GPU, a 7B model is the safe baseline. It is matching parameter size to memory. If the GPU has 24 GB or more, a 13B model becomes reasonable. If the GPU has only 8 GB, then smaller or aggressively quantized models are required. Engineering discipline starts here.

Comparing Two Practical Candidates

Next, we will now compare two realistic candidates for a private deployment:

- Meta Llama 2 7B
- Technology Innovation Institute Falcon-7B

Both of these are 7B class models and have been widely adopted. However, the licensing and intended usage differ. The Llama 2 uses a community license that permits commercial usage under certain conditions. Whereasm the Falcon-7B uses Apache 2.0, which is more permissive. Hence, for many enterprises, the Apache 2.0 simplifies compliance review.

We will now move on to the hardware. Both the 7B models can run on a 16 GB GPU in FP16 mode using vLLM, and they can run comfortably in quantized modes if memory pressure appears. Therefore, for our current assumption of a 16 GB GPU and internal-only deployment, either model is feasible. If licensing simplicity is a priority, the Falcon-7B is attractive. If ecosystem familiarity and instruction tuning strength matter more, then the Llama 2 7B Instruct becomes a strong candidate.

For this demonstration, we will choose Llama 2 7B Instruct because of its strong instruction-following behavior and widespread documentation. There is nothing to worry as the process remains the same for Falcon-7B too.

Recording Model Decision

To start with, we will first document the reasoning within the following file:

```
docs/model_selection.md
```

Inside it, we will then write:

- Hardware available: 1 GPU, 16 GB VRAM
- Target workload: batch summarization and extraction
- License accepted: Llama 2 Community License
- Selected model: Llama-2-7b-chat

At any later stage, if someone upgrades hardware, they will understand why we chose 7B rather than 13B.

Downloading and Storing Model Weights

Next, we will now retrieve the weights from Hugging Face using the standard CLI:

```
huggingface-cli download meta-llama/Llama-2-7b-chat-hf --
local-dir ./tmp_llama2_7b
```

This command downloads the model files locally. We move them into our controlled offline asset's structure.

Here, our asset's structure should look like this:

```
private-ai-spark/
  assets/
```

```
models/
  llama2_7b_chat/
    weights/
    manifest.json
```

After this, we move the downloaded weights:

```
mkdir -p assets/models/llama2_7b_chat/weights
mv ./tmp_llama2_7b/* assets/models/llama2_7b_chat/weights/
```

We will now create a small manifest file that documents origin and checksum as shown below:

```
{
  "model_name": "Llama-2-7b-chat-hf",
  "source": "https://huggingface.co/meta-llama/Llama-2-7b-
chat-hf",
  "license": "Llama 2 Community License",
  "download_date": "2026-02-20",
  "hardware_target": "16GB GPU",
  "notes": "Selected for instruction tuning and internal
summarization tasks."
}
```

We can also compute SHA256 checksums for the main weight files and add them to this manifest. This makes our deployment reproducible.

Pointing vLLM to Offline Weights

Finally, we start the vLLM using the local path:

```
vllm serve assets/models/llama2_7b_chat/weights --host 0.0.0.0
--port 8000
```

This command loads weights directly from our offline directory. vLLM does not need internet access. The Spark will call the same internal endpoint as before. The only difference is that the model is now fully under our infrastructure control.

Overall, the Spark continues to orchestrate batch requests, and the vLLM continues to serve inference efficiently. The model is also in our controlled assets directory with documented provenance. Such alignment of hardware, licensing, storage, and serving is what makes private AI sustainable rather than fragile.

Spark-to-vLLM Batch Calls

We now have three important building blocks in place:

- The Spark prepares chunked prompts and stores them as a clean table.
- vLLM runs as an internal inference service behind a stable endpoint. And,
- Our model weights live inside our offline assets directory and are versioned.

The missing piece is the connector, basically a disciplined module that can allow the Spark to send requests to vLLM in batches, capture responses, record trace fields, and write everything back into a structured DataFrame. This topic is about building that bridge properly.

So here, we will not write ad-hoc loops or call the model row by row in the driver. Instead, we will process requests per partition so Spark keeps control of distribution, and we will attach trace metadata so every response remains explainable.

Design Principles

However, before we implement anything, we clarify three rules.

- The first one is that there will be one Spark partition that manages its own small HTTP session. That reduces overhead and keeps network behavior predictable.

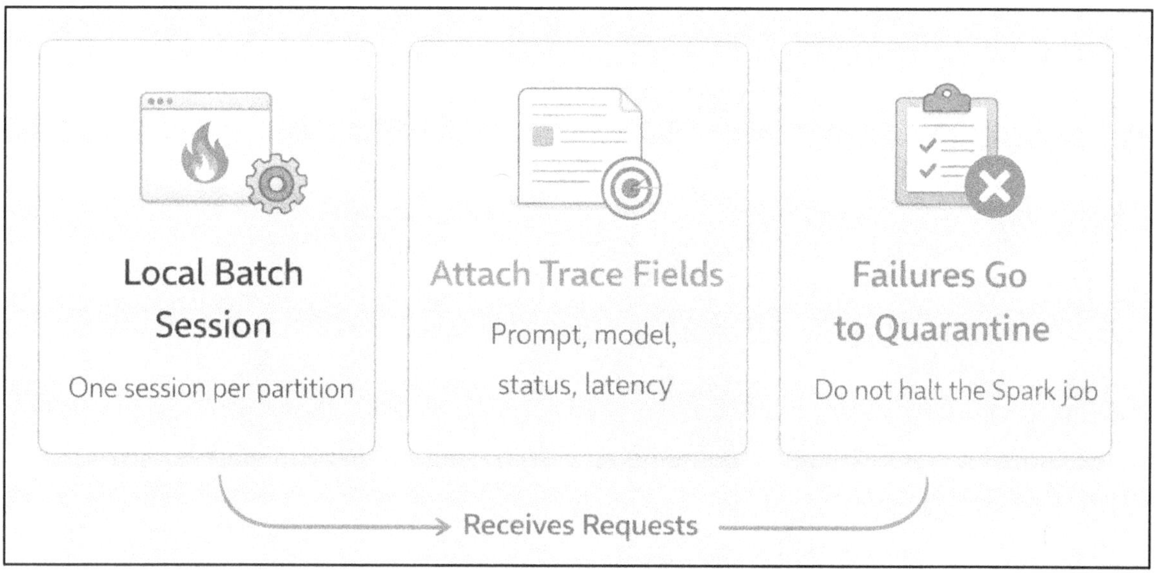

Fig 6.4 Spark-vLLM Design Principles

- The second is that, every response row must contain trace fields such as

prompt_version, **model_name**, **status_code**, and **latency_ms**. These fields make debugging practical.

- And the third one is that, the failures must not stop the batch. Instead, the failures will be marked and written to a quarantine table exactly as we did in earlier chapters.

With these rules in mind, we implement one small module.

Create Dedicated Batch Caller Module

To begin with, we will first create a new file **src/mailroom/llm/batch_call.py** and will try to keep it compact and focused.

And now, we will start with the imports and configuration constants.

```
# batch_call.py - block 1
import requests
import time
from typing import Iterator
```

After this, we will define a helper that sends a single request and returns structured results. Basically, we need to capture the raw JSON string so downstream jobs can interpret it safely.

```
# batch_call.py - block 2
def call_vllm(prompt_text: str, base_url: str, api_key: str,
model_name: str):
    headers = {"Authorization": f"Bearer {api_key}"}
    payload = {
        "model": model_name,
        "messages": [{"role": "user", "content":
prompt_text}],
        "temperature": 0.0
    }
    start = time.time()
    try:
        r = requests.post(
            f"{base_url}/v1/chat/completions",
            json=payload,
```

```
            headers=headers,
            timeout=60
        )
        latency_ms = int((time.time() - start) * 1000)
        return r.status_code, r.text, latency_ms, None
    except Exception as e:
        latency_ms = int((time.time() - start) * 1000)
        return 0, "", latency_ms, str(e)
```

This above function never throws outward and it always return the structured output.

Partition-Level Processing

Next, we will try to define the function Spark will execute per partition. Now here, each partition will reuse the same HTTP session logic and iterate over rows sequentially. This keeps memory stable and avoids concurrency complexity in our beginner workflow.

```
# batch_call.py - block 3
def process_partition(
    rows: Iterator,
    base_url: str,
    api_key: str,
    model_name: str
):
    for row in rows:
        status, body, latency_ms, error_msg = call_vllm(
            row.prompt_text,
            base_url,
            api_key,
            model_name
        )
        yield (
            row.file_path,
```

```
            int(row.chunk_id),
            row.prompt_version,
            model_name,
            int(status),
            int(latency_ms),
            body,
            error_msg
        )
```

This function is intentionally linear such that each row produces one output row.

Integrate into Spark Job

After this, we will now create a Spark job **src/mailroom/llm/llm_batch_job.py** that uses the following module:

```
# llm_batch_job.py - block 1
from pyspark.sql import SparkSession
from pyspark.sql.types import (
    StructType, StructField,
    StringType, IntegerType
)
from src.mailroom.llm.batch_call import process_partition
spark =
SparkSession.builder.appName("SparkToVLLMBatch").getOrCreate()
run_date = "2026-02-20"
input_path = f"data/gold/llm_prep/{run_date}/"
output_path = f"data/gold/llm_results/{run_date}/"
quarantine_path = "data/quarantine/llm_calls/"
df = spark.read.parquet(input_path)
print("Rows prepared for LLM:", df.count())
```

Next, we will now define the connection settings. In production, these would come from configuration.

```
# llm_batch_job.py - block 2
BASE_URL = "http://vllm-internal:8000"
API_KEY = "token-abc123"
MODEL_NAME = "llama2_7b_chat"
```

Next, is to define the output schema clearly.

```
# llm_batch_job.py - block 3
result_schema = StructType([
    StructField("file_path", StringType(), True),
    StructField("chunk_id", IntegerType(), True),
    StructField("prompt_version", StringType(), True),
    StructField("model_name", StringType(), True),
    StructField("status_code", IntegerType(), True),
    StructField("latency_ms", IntegerType(), True),
    StructField("response_text", StringType(), True),
    StructField("error_message", StringType(), True),
])
```

We will now apply the partition processing.

```
# llm_batch_job.py - block 4
rdd = df.rdd.mapPartitions(
    lambda rows: process_partition(
        rows,
        BASE_URL,
        API_KEY,
        MODEL_NAME
    )
)
results_df = spark.createDataFrame(rdd, schema=result_schema)
```

This keeps the Spark fully in control of parallelism.

Split Success and Failure

Now here, we will treat it exactly like earlier quarantine patterns.

```
# llm_batch_job.py - block 5
success_df = results_df.filter(results_df.status_code == 200)
failure_df = results_df.filter(results_df.status_code != 200)
```

After this, we will then write the successful responses:

```
success_df.write.mode("overwrite").parquet(output_path)
print("Successful calls:", success_df.count())
```

And will write the failures too:

```
failure_df.write.mode("append").parquet(quarantine_path)
print("Failed calls:", failure_df.count())
```

After all such tasks, our Spark job can now produce the structured inference outputs and preserves the failures for inspection.

Trace Fields

If we could observe, each of the row contains the following columns:

```
file_path
chunk_id
prompt_version
model_name
status_code
latency_ms
```

These above fields give us full traceability. If a summary looks wrong, we can trace it to a specific chunk, prompt version, and model. If latency spikes, we can query average **`latency_ms`** per run. If errors increase, we can count failure reasons. This keeps vLLM integration aligned with our private AI philosophy: measurable, auditable, and repeatable.

This whole process of separation of roles keeps the system scalable without becoming complex, and it maintains the same discipline we applied throughout the project.

Performance Measurement and Comparison

Until now, we built two very different paths to produce summaries, in which one path was our baseline extractive method that used sentence ranking and keyword overlap, and it ran entirely inside Spark without any model server. Whereas, the second path prepared chunked prompts, sent them to an internal vLLM service, and stored structured responses with trace fields. At this point, we do not rely on intuition to decide which path is "better."

We measure first. The concept of performance measurement does not mean tuning. It means observing throughput and latency in a consistent way and storing those observations so we can compare runs later. In this topic, we will compare a local transformer inference setup against our vLLM setup for the same summarization workload, and we will record metrics per run so the comparison becomes part of our data, not just a conversation.

Identify Metrics

Before writing any code, we decide what performance means in our context. For summarization workloads, two numbers matter most:

- ***Throughput*** which tells how many chunks per second we process
- ***Latency*** speaks how long one chunk takes on average

So here, we will compute:

- Total chunks processed
- Total elapsed time
- Average latency per chunk
- Chunks per second

We will keep the math simple. The Spark already gives us row counts. We will measure wall-clock time in Python which is enough for meaningful comparison at this level.

Since we did not implement local transformer inference earlier in this book, so here, we will define a local transformer directly inside a Python process without the vLLM batching. And we will assume that the setup processes one chunk at a time, does not use continuous batching and we will assume the same model, hardware, summarization prompts and number of chunks.

In addition, we will consider the local transformer numbers as a baseline measurement.

Measure vLLM Performance

To start with, we will first return to **`llm_batch_job.py`**. Since, we already captured the **`latency_ms`** per request, so here, we add a simple timing block around the full batch execution.

Hence, at the top of the job:

```
import time
start_time = time.time()
```

And, after writing results:

```
end_time = time.time()
elapsed_seconds = end_time - start_time
```

We will now compute the simple aggregates from the result DataFrame.

```
total_chunks = results_df.count()
avg_latency =
results_df.groupBy().avg("latency_ms").collect()[0][0]
throughput = total_chunks / elapsed_seconds if elapsed_seconds
> 0 else 0
print("Total chunks:", total_chunks)
print("Elapsed seconds:", elapsed_seconds)
print("Average latency (ms):", avg_latency)
print("Throughput (chunks/sec):", throughput)
```

After calculating, it gives us a clear performance profile for the vLLM run.

Record Metrics

Next, we will store these metrics so we can compare across runs. For this, we will add a small metrics write block:

```
from pyspark.sql.functions import current_timestamp
metrics_row = spark.createDataFrame([{
    "run_date": run_date,
    "model_name": MODEL_NAME,
    "engine": "vllm",
    "total_chunks": int(total_chunks),
    "elapsed_seconds": float(elapsed_seconds),
```

```
    "avg_latency_ms": float(avg_latency),
    "throughput_chunks_per_sec": float(throughput)
}]).withColumn("logged_at", current_timestamp())
metrics_row.write.mode("append").parquet("runs/performance_met
rics")
```

With this, now every batch run leaves behind a performance snapshot.

Simulated Local Transformer Baseline

In the beginning, we already assumed that a local transformer baseline processed the same number of chunks without vLLM batching. So here, let us assume that we have measured the following:

- Total chunks: 1,000
- Total time: 600 seconds
- Average latency: 580 ms
- Throughput: 1.66 chunks/sec

After this, we record them in the same metrics table but we do this using a different engine label.

```
baseline_metrics = spark.createDataFrame([{
    "run_date": run_date,
    "model_name": MODEL_NAME,
    "engine": "local_transformer",
    "total_chunks": 1000,
    "elapsed_seconds": 600.0,
    "avg_latency_ms": 580.0,
    "throughput_chunks_per_sec": 1.66
}]).withColumn("logged_at", current_timestamp())
baseline_metrics.write.mode("append").parquet("runs/performanc
e_metrics")
```

After this, both the engine types live in the same table.

Query and Compare inside Spark

Next is to query the comparisons directly as shown below:

```
perf_df = spark.read.parquet("runs/performance_metrics")
```

```
perf_df.filter(perf_df.run_date == run_date).show()
```

In this, we can also compute the relative improvement:

```
from pyspark.sql.functions import col

vllm_df = perf_df.filter((col("run_date") == run_date) &
(col("engine") == "vllm"))

local_df = perf_df.filter((col("run_date") == run_date) &
(col("engine") == "local_transformer"))

joined = vllm_df.crossJoin(local_df)

comparison = joined.select(

    (col("vllm.throughput_chunks_per_sec") /
col("local_transformer.throughput_chunks_per_sec")).alias("thr
oughput_multiplier")

)

comparison.show()
```

After all this, we now have a measurable comparison which is without complex benchmarking frameworks.

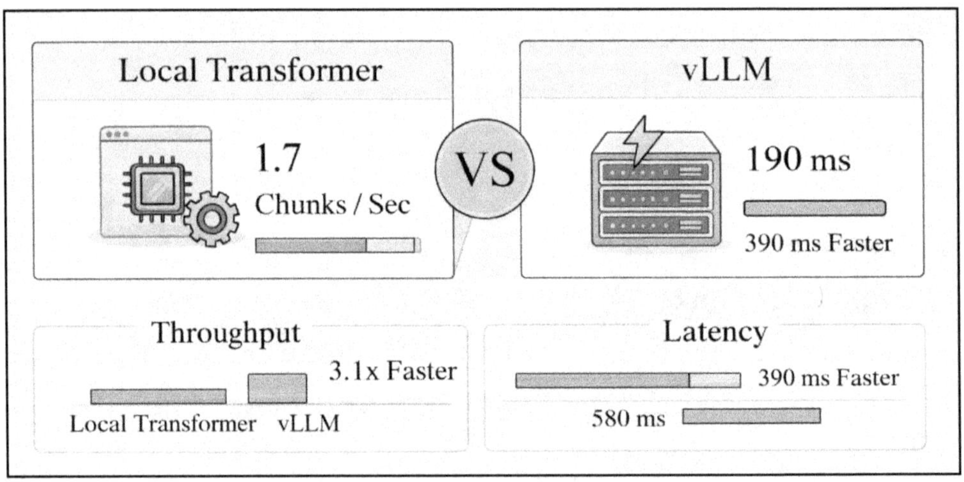

Fig 6.5 Performance Comparison

If you could see the above comparison, the vLLM often shows higher throughput for multi-request workloads because it uses continuous batching and optimized memory management. A local transformer setup without batching may show similar per-request latency but lower overall throughput when processing many chunks. This is exactly why Spark plus vLLM complement each other. The Spark distributes the requests. And, the vLLM batches them efficiently on the

GPU. The combination increases total chunks processed per second without requiring complex manual optimization inside Spark.

Storing Metrics Run-wise

We must always make a note that the performance changes over time. And the GPU drivers also change. Hence, it is bound that the model versions will change with time or a particular period. So here, if we only measure once and never store results, we lose the ability to compare runs objectively.

Engine	Chunks	Time (sec)	Avg. Latency	Throughput
Local Transformer	1,000	600	580 ms	1.7 / sec
vLLM	1,000	190	190 ms	5.2 / sec

Fig 6.6 Run Metrics

So, if we could write performance metrics within our site **`runs/performance_metrics`**, then we could certainly build a historical record. Later, if someone upgrades to a 13B model or changes chunk size, we can measure again and compare across run dates.

With this, we all implemented the performance measurement using simple wall-clock timing and per-request latency capture. We calculated throughput and average latency for our vLLM batch job and stored results as structured rows in a metrics table. We also simulated a local transformer baseline and recorded it in the same format, enabling side-by-side comparison inside Spark.

Summary

In this chapter we extended our private AI architecture by introducing vLLM as an internal inference engine that complemented Spark rather than replacing it. We selected a local model based on hardware constraints and licensing considerations, documented the reasoning, and stored the weights inside our offline assets structure with a manifest file. We then implemented Spark-to-vLLM batch calls per partition, captured structured trace fields such as model name, prompt version, latency, and status codes, and wrote both successful and failed calls into structured tables. Failures were treated as data rather than interruptions, reinforcing our quarantine pattern.

We then measured performance instead of assuming it. We captured wall-clock time, average latency per request, and overall throughput for the vLLM workflow, and we recorded these metrics as structured rows in a performance table. We compared these measurements with an assumed local transformer baseline to illustrate how continuous batching can improve throughput. By storing metrics per run, we turned performance into historical data rather than a one-time observation. This whole thing completed the architectural picture wherein the Spark orchestrated, the vLLM accelerated, and the measurements verified behavior.

CHAPTER 7: PACKAGING PRIVATE AI

Overview

In this chapter, we'll move from building capability to packaging it for real use. It'll take ingestion, model training, scoring, summarization, optional LLM calls, and reporting, and combine them into a single pipeline that you can run with one command and one configuration file. The first thing you'll do is define a consistent run-date convention so each execution writes outputs into structured directories. Then, we'll introduce lightweight scheduling patterns for daily or weekly automation. With this, you won't have to rely on memory or manual steps. It'll be easy to create a repeatable execution flow that can be triggered reliably in controlled environments.

As the chapter goes on, we'll add optimal monitoring so each run records how long the job takes, how many errors there are, and how big the output is. It'll also generate a short run report that's good for sharing with stakeholders. After that, we'll look at how to adapt the project to new datasets. You'll learn how to identify which modules stay the same, like schema contracts and logging formats, and which modules need to change, like parsers, labels, and prompt templates. By the time we reach the end of the chapter, we'll have a solid understanding of how to take a working private AI pipeline and transform it into a packaged, scheduled, monitored, and reusable system that can evolve beyond its original dataset.

Single Command Workflow

Until thus far of these six chapters, we built the capabilities carefully. We ingested emails, we parsed them into a stable schema, we cleaned defensively, we trained a baseline classifier, we extracted keywords, we generated summaries, we optionally accelerated inference with vLLM, we logged everything and we measured performance too. All of this worked, but right now our system still feels like a collection of scripts. A real system feels repeatable. It feels like something you can run with one clear command and trust that it will execute the correct sequence in the correct order with the correct configuration.

In this topic, we will package our private mailroom assistant into a single-command workflow. We will not introduce heavy orchestration frameworks. We will not bring in complex schedulers. We will simply wrap ingestion, training, scoring, summarization, reporting, and LLM steps behind a small driver module that reads one configuration file and executes a defined pipeline.

We will now work that out in the following:

Packaging Layer

Until now, we ran individual jobs like:

```
normalize_emails_job.py
train_classifier_job.py
```

```
batch_scoring_job.py
summary_baseline_job.py
llm_batch_job.py
reporting_job.py
```

This above thing worked during development.

However, if another engineer joins the team, they should not have to memorize execution order. And, if we deploy this into a controlled environment, the operators should not manually decide which script to run next.

So here, we will build that packaging layer which can offer us:

- Deterministic order
- Single source of configuration
- Reproducible runs
- Reduced cognitive load

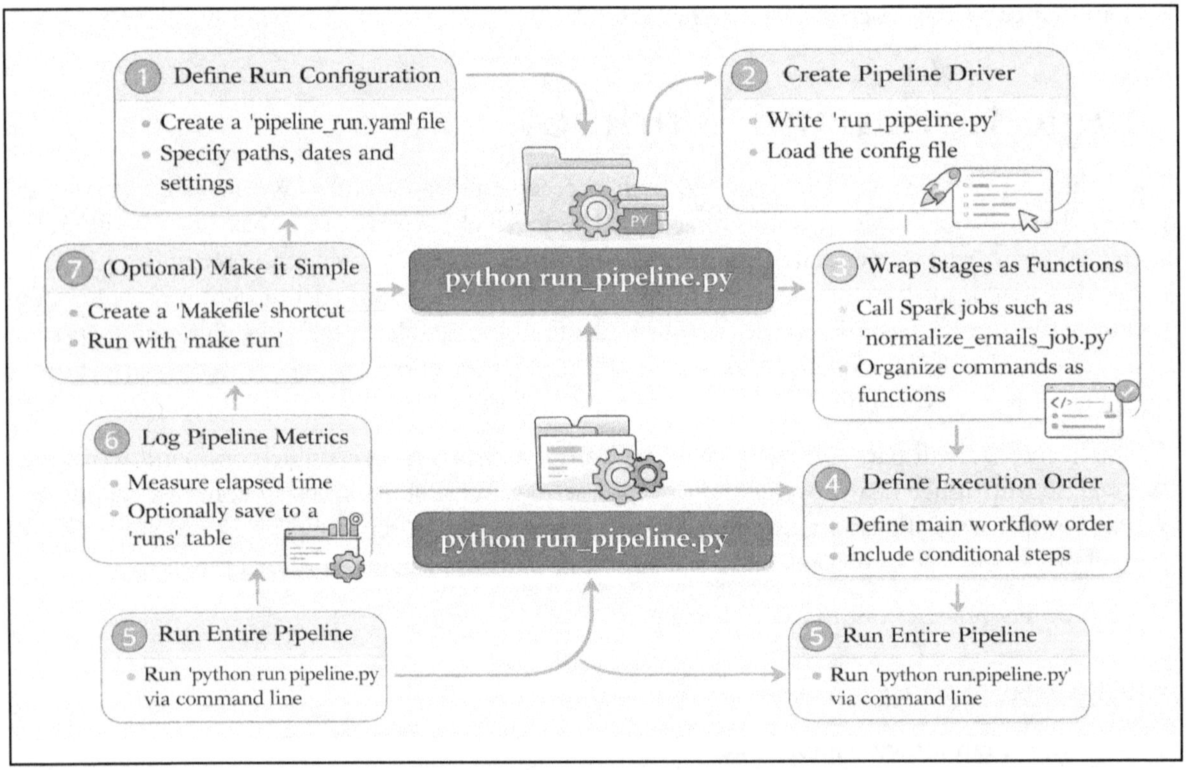

Fig 7.1 Layers of Packaging

Define Unified Run

To start with, we will first create a single configuration file that describes a full run:

```
run_date: "2026-02-20"
paths:
  raw_input: "assets/datasets/enron_sample/raw/"
  normalized_output: "data/silver/emails_normalized/"
  tagged_output: "data/gold/emails_tagged/"
  summary_output: "data/gold/emails_summaries/"
  report_output: "data/gold/reports/"
llm:
  enabled: true
  prep_output: "data/gold/llm_prep/"
  result_output: "data/gold/llm_results/"
model:
  classifier_version: "baseline_v1"
  llm_model_name: "llama2_7b_chat"
```

This will be saved in **configs/pipeline_run.yaml** file which will now become our single control plane for a batch run.

Create Pipeline Driver Module

We first create **src/mailroom/pipeline/run_pipeline.py**.

And within it, we will load the following configuration:

```
import yaml
import subprocess
def load_config(path):
    with open(path) as f:
        return yaml.safe_load(f)
cfg = load_config("configs/pipeline_run.yaml")
run_date = cfg["run_date"]
```

With this, we now have the run date and configuration in memory.

Wrap Stages as Function Call

We don't need to duplicate logic. We just call the existing Spark jobs using **`spark-submit`**. This keeps packaging simple and respects our earlier code.

- Ingestion and Normalization

```
def run_normalization():
    subprocess.run([
        "spark-submit",
        "src/mailroom/ingestion/normalize_emails_job.py",
        run_date
    ], check=True)
```

- Training

```
def run_training():
    subprocess.run([
        "spark-submit",
        "src/mailroom/ml/train_classifier_job.py",
        run_date
    ], check=True)
```

- Batch Scoring

```
def run_scoring():
    subprocess.run([
        "spark-submit",
        "src/mailroom/ml/batch_scoring_job.py",
        run_date
    ], check=True)
```

- Baseline Summaries

```
def run_baseline_summary():
    subprocess.run([
```

```
        "spark-submit",
        "src/mailroom/nlp/summary_baseline_job.py",
        run_date
    ], check=True)
```

- LLM Preparation and Calls

```
def run_llm_steps():
    subprocess.run([
        "spark-submit",
        "src/mailroom/nlp/llm_prep_job.py",
        "configs/llm_prep.yaml"
    ], check=True)
    subprocess.run([
        "spark-submit",
        "src/mailroom/llm/llm_batch_job.py"
    ], check=True)
```

- Reporting

```
def run_reporting():
    subprocess.run([
        "spark-submit",
        "src/mailroom/reporting/reporting_job.py",
        run_date
    ], check=True)
```

Define Execution Order

After the wrapping of stages, we will now define the main flow.

```
def main():
    print("Starting Private Mailroom Pipeline for:", run_date)
    run_normalization()
```

```
    run_training()
    run_scoring()
    run_baseline_summary()
    if cfg["llm"]["enabled"]:
        run_llm_steps()
    run_reporting()
    print("Pipeline completed successfully.")
if __name__ == "__main__":
    main()
```

This file now becomes the heart of our packaging layer.

Run 'One Command' System

And we are done, we simply have to execute:

```
python src/mailroom/pipeline/run_pipeline.py
```

This above single command triggers:

1. Ingestion
2. Model training
3. Batch scoring
4. Baseline summarization
5. Optional LLM acceleration
6. Reporting

And, the operator does not need to remember internal job ordering too.

With this, we have successfully transformed our private mailroom assistant from a collection of individual Spark jobs into a packaged workflow controlled by a single configuration file and a single command. The whole pipeline is now cohesive, repeatable, and ready for real operational usage. The Spark continues to execute each stage, vLLM remains optional, and configuration governs behavior. This is the moment where our private AI stops being a development artifact and becomes a deployable system.

Scheduling Routine Runs

Up to this point, we have built a capable system and wrapped it behind a single command. That was a major shift. However, a system that runs only when someone remembers to execute it is still fragile. The concept of Private AI really becomes highly valuable when it turns into a routine.

In a mailroom scenario, the emails arrive every day, every hour and everty minute. The summaries should refresh daily, at the least. The reports should be generated consistently, if possible. And, the metrics must accumulate over the time.

Hence, in this topic, we will now make a move from manual execution to scheduled execution. So here, we will define a clear pattern for daily and weekly runs, we will enforce explicit input and output directories for each run, and we will record a manifest for every scheduled execution so traceability remains intact.

Need of Scheduling

Many teams build AI pipelines but never formalize their execution pattern. The result is drift. One week a run happens manually, and another week it is skipped. Someone changes an input path, and then someone forgets to rotate outputs, and soon the whole system becomes unreliable.

So, in this topic, we do not aim to teach you a heavy orchestration tool. Rather, our goal is to define a clean scheduling discipline, which has:

- A fixed run cadence
- Explicit run dates
- Deterministic input paths
- Deterministic output paths
- A recorded run manifest

And, when these above elements exist, the routine execution becomes safe and predictable.

Run Date Convention

We already use **run_date** in our configuration. Now we formalize its meaning.

Daily pattern:

```
run_date = YYYY-MM-DD
```

Weekly pattern:

```
run_date = YYYY-WW
```

We will treat each scheduled run as a separate folder under our data directories. For example:

```
data/gold/emails_tagged/2026-02-20/
data/gold/emails_summaries/2026-02-20/
data/gold/reports/2026-02-20/
```

This prevents accidental overwriting and ensures historical reproducibility.

Scheduled Config Template

Instead of editing the main config manually each day, we create a template file:

```
configs/pipeline_template.yaml
```

Example:

```
run_date: "__AUTO__"
paths:
  raw_input: "assets/datasets/enron_sample/raw/"
  base_output: "data/gold/"
llm:
  enabled: true
model:
  classifier_version: "baseline_v1"
```

Now we generate a concrete config for each scheduled run.

Small Scheduler Wrapper Script

Create:

```
scripts/run_daily.sh
```

Example content:

```
#!/bin/bash
RUN_DATE=$(date +%Y-%m-%d)
cp configs/pipeline_template.yaml configs/pipeline_run.yaml
sed -i "s/__AUTO__/${RUN_DATE}/g" configs/pipeline_run.yaml
python src/mailroom/pipeline/run_pipeline.py
```

This script automatically injects today's date into the run configuration. The pipeline driver already respects **run_date**, so all outputs become date-scoped automatically.

For weekly runs:

```
RUN_DATE=$(date +%Y-W%V)
```

This simple change supports weekly aggregation patterns.

Explicit Input and Output Directories

Inside **run_pipeline.py**, we now make directory construction deterministic.

Instead of hardcoding full paths, we construct them using **run_date**.

Example adjustment:

```
base_output = cfg["paths"]["base_output"]
normalized_path =
f"{base_output}/emails_normalized/{run_date}/"
tagged_path = f"{base_output}/emails_tagged/{run_date}/"
summary_path = f"{base_output}/emails_summaries/{run_date}/"
report_path = f"{base_output}/reports/{run_date}/"
```

Now every stage writes into a clearly namespaced folder. No stage overwrites another run. The directory tree itself becomes documentation.

Cron Job for Automation

Now we schedule the script.

Open cron:

```
crontab -e
```

Add a daily run at 2 AM:

```
0 2 * * * /path/to/project/scripts/run_daily.sh >>
logs/pipeline.log 2>&1
```

This means:

- Run every day
- Capture stdout and stderr
- Append logs

For weekly execution on Sundays:

```
0 3 * * 0 /path/to/project/scripts/run_daily.sh >>
logs/pipeline.log 2>&1
```

We now have routine automation without introducing complex infrastructure.

Generate and Store a Run Manifest

Every scheduled run should produce a manifest file that documents:

- run_date
- input directory
- output directories
- model version
- llm enabled flag
- timestamp

At the end of **run_pipeline.py**, add:

```
import json
from datetime import datetime
manifest = {
    "run_date": run_date,
    "input_path": cfg["paths"]["raw_input"],
    "base_output": base_output,
    "classifier_version": cfg["model"]["classifier_version"],
    "llm_enabled": cfg["llm"]["enabled"],
    "timestamp": datetime.utcnow().isoformat()
}
manifest_path = f"runs/manifests/{run_date}.json"
with open(manifest_path, "w") as f:
    json.dump(manifest, f, indent=2)
print("Run manifest written to:", manifest_path)
```

Now each scheduled run leaves behind a manifest record.

After several months later, if someone asks:

- Which model produced this summary?
- Was LLM enabled that day?

- What input directory was used?
- When exactly did the run execute?

The manifest can sufficiently answer these above questions immediately.

Our private mailroom assistant is no longer a one-time pipeline. It is now a routine system that runs predictably, writes outputs into structured directories, and documents itself every time it executes.

Optimized Monitoring

We have now packaged our private mailroom assistant and scheduled it to run daily or weekly. That is a strong step. However, a scheduled system without visibility is still risky. If one day the job takes twice as long, or if error counts spike, or if output size suddenly drops, we should not discover that weeks later. At the same time, we do not want to introduce heavy monitoring stacks or complex observability platforms. For our scale and audience, optimal monitoring is enough.

The concept of optimal monitoring means we measure only three things consistently that includes the total job duration, total error count, and total output size. And then, we publish a compact run report that can be shared with stakeholders without exposing internal logs.

The objective of this topic is not to build enterprise-grade monitoring, rather just to embed simple operational awareness directly into our pipeline.

Capture Total Job Duration

We have already measured elapsed time in earlier topics. So here, we formalize it inside the pipeline driver.

So here, we go to **run_pipeline.py** and at the beginning of **main()** we capture start time:

```
import time
start_time = time.time()
```

And, at the end of the pipeline execution:

```
end_time = time.time()
job_duration_seconds = end_time - start_time
print("Total job duration (seconds):", job_duration_seconds)
```

This number now becomes part of our monitoring metrics.

Capture Error Counts across Stages

We are already writing the quarantine tables for failed LLM calls and other failures. But now, we will also collect the error counts in one place.

For this, at the end of the pipeline, we will query the Spark for error metrics as shown below:

```
from pyspark.sql import SparkSession
spark = SparkSession.builder.getOrCreate()
run_date = cfg["run_date"]
llm_quarantine_path = "data/quarantine/llm_calls/"
summary_quarantine_path = "data/quarantine/summaries/"
llm_errors = 0
summary_errors = 0
if cfg["llm"]["enabled"]:
    try:
        llm_errors = spark.read.parquet(llm_quarantine_path) \
            .filter(f"run_date = '{run_date}'").count()
    except:
        llm_errors = 0
try:
    summary_errors =
spark.read.parquet(summary_quarantine_path) \
        .filter(f"run_date = '{run_date}'").count()
except:
    summary_errors = 0
total_errors = llm_errors + summary_errors
print("Total errors:", total_errors)
```

Wafter running it, we will have a single aggregated error count for each run.

Capture Output Sizes

The output size is a powerful signal. And, somehowe if the tagged dataset usually contains 10,000 records and suddenly it contains just 500, then we can say that something is wrong.

So, for this, we will capture the record counts from key outputs:

```
tagged_path = f"data/gold/emails_tagged/{run_date}/"
summary_path = f"data/gold/emails_summaries/{run_date}/"
report_path = f"data/gold/reports/{run_date}/"
tagged_count = spark.read.parquet(tagged_path).count()
summary_count = spark.read.parquet(summary_path).count()
report_count = spark.read.parquet(report_path).count()
print("Tagged rows:", tagged_count)
print("Summary rows:", summary_count)
print("Report rows:", report_count)
```

These counts serve as output size indicators.

Store Monitoring Metrics

Next, we will now combine the duration, error count, and output counts into a structured monitoring record.

```
from pyspark.sql.functions import current_timestamp
monitor_row = spark.createDataFrame([{
    "run_date": run_date,
    "job_duration_seconds": float(job_duration_seconds),
    "total_errors": int(total_errors),
    "tagged_count": int(tagged_count),
    "summary_count": int(summary_count),
    "report_count": int(report_count)
}]).withColumn("logged_at", current_timestamp())
monitor_row.write.mode("append").parquet("runs/monitoring_metr
ics")
print("Monitoring metrics written.")
```

After this, each scheduled run leaves behind a monitoring record.

Create Run Report

The stakeholders rarely want to inspect Parquet tables, rather they want a simple summary.

So here, we will generate a compact JSON report for each run.

```
import json
from datetime import datetime
run_report = {
    "run_date": run_date,
    "completed_at": datetime.utcnow().isoformat(),
    "job_duration_seconds": job_duration_seconds,
    "total_errors": total_errors,
    "outputs": {
        "tagged_rows": tagged_count,
        "summary_rows": summary_count,
        "report_rows": report_count
    }
}
report_file = f"runs/reports/{run_date}_run_report.json"
with open(report_file, "w") as f:
    json.dump(run_report, f, indent=2)
print("Run report generated at:", report_file)
```

This file can be shared directly with stakeholders.

If the stakeholders prefer spreadsheets, we can export a one-row CSV.

```
monitor_row.coalesce(1).write.mode("overwrite") \
    .option("header", "true") \
    .csv(f"exports/run_report_{run_date}.csv")
```

At any given point of time, if stakeholders ask for a status update, we run the JSON and CSV report and can provide to the stakeholders instantly.

With this, the private mailroom assistant now runs routinely, documents itself, and reports its health without requiring heavy infrastructure.

New Dataset Calibration

We built the private mailroom assistant using a curated subset of the Enron email dataset. However, the value of this system does not lie in this Enron dataset itself. The value lies in the architecture we constructed around it. If our system only works for one dataset, then we built a demo. But, if it adapts cleanly to new datasets, then we can say that we have built a reusable private AI framework.

So, in this final topic of this closure chapter, we will clearly separate what remains constant and what must change when adapting to a new dataset.

Separate Architectures

Before touching any code, we must state a principle, which is that ***data changes, but architecture should not***. When moving to a new dataset, we do not rewrite ingestion, training, scoring, reporting, monitoring, and scheduling. Instead, we modify only the dataset-facing modules.

In the following, I will show you to divide our system into two layers:

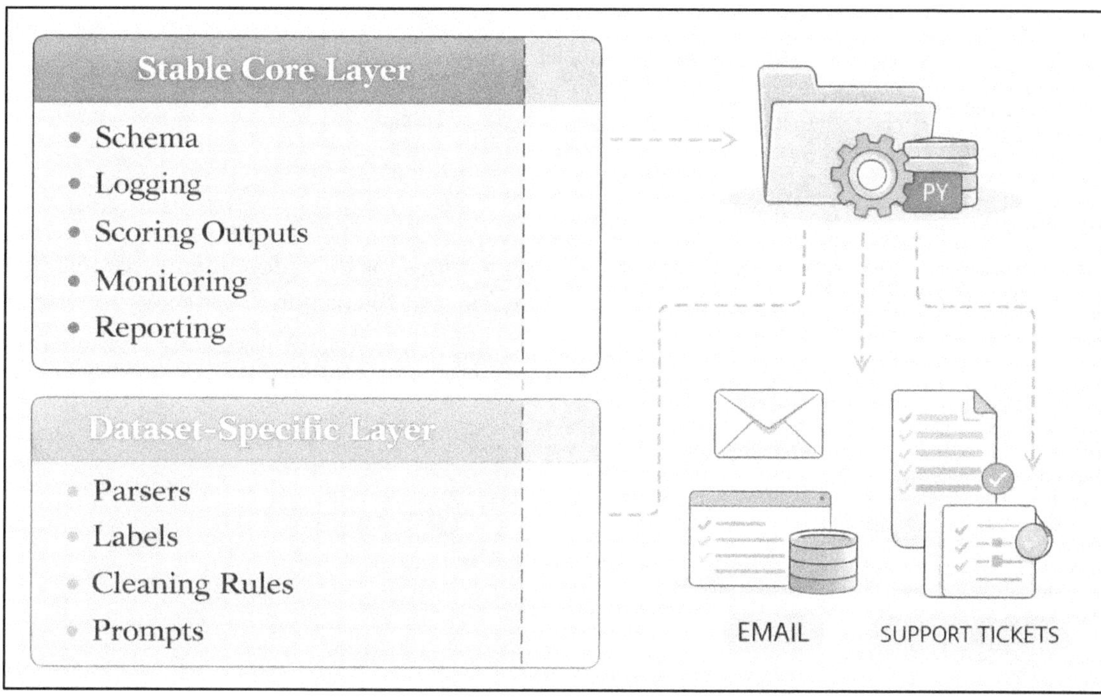

Fig 7.2 Stable vs. Dataset-specific Layers

The **Stable Core Layer** includes:

- Schema contract
- Logging format

- Batch scoring structure
- Output directory conventions
- Monitoring metrics
- Manifest structure
- Spark-to-vLLM integration

And, the **Dataset-Specific Layer** comprises of:

- Raw file parser
- Label taxonomy
- Prompt templates
- Feature assumptions
- Cleaning rules

Once we understand this boundary, the adaptation becomes predictable rather than chaotic.

What Remains Constant?

Our internal canonical schema looks like this:

- ***file_path***
- sender
- recipients
- ***sent_at***
- subject
- body

Even if the new dataset comes from support tickets, chat logs, or PDF documents, we map them into this canonical shape. That mapping is the responsibility of the parser. Everything downstream remains unchanged.

The classifier expects:

- text column
- label column

The summarizer expects:

- subject
- body
- keywords

The reporting layer expects:

- tag
- timestamp

All these above expectations do not change in the canonical schema.

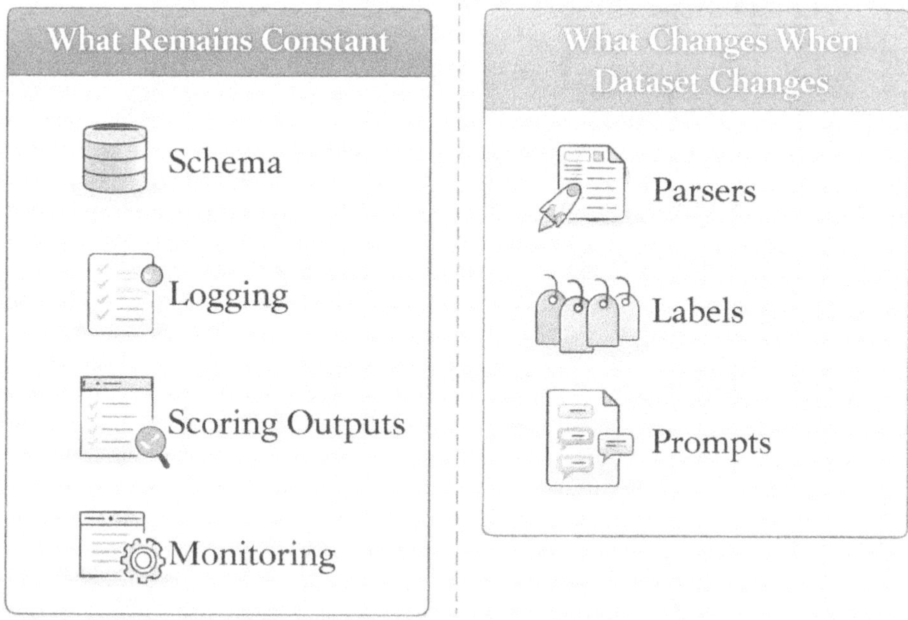

Fig 7.3 Constant vs. Dynamic Structures

Our logging system records:

- ***run_date***
- ***model_version***
- ***prompt_version***
- error counts
- job duration

This structure remains constant regardless of dataset. We do not rewrite logging when switching datasets.

The classifier output always produces:

- ***predicted_tag***
- ***confidence_score***

The summarizer always produces ***baseline_summary***.

The LLM layer always produces:

- ***response_text***
- ***status_code***
- ***latency_ms***

These structural contracts remain stable.

What Changes with Dataset?

We will now look at what must change. Suppose we move from emails to support tickets in CSV format.

For example, previously it is **normalize_emails_job.py**

And later, we create **normalize_support_tickets_job.py**

The job still outputs the canonical schema. Only the extraction logic changes.

Just lok at the following adjustment:

```
df_raw = spark.read.csv("assets/datasets/support/raw/", header=True)

df_normalized = df_raw.select(
    col("ticket_id").alias("file_path"),
    col("customer_email").alias("sender"),
    lit("").alias("recipients"),
    col("created_at").alias("sent_at"),
    col("subject"),
    col("description").alias("body")
)
```

The downstream jobs remain untouched.

For emails, we used:

- HR
- Finance
- Legal
- Ops
- Personal

For support tickets, the labels might be:

- Billing
- Technical
- Account
- Cancellation

We just have to update the labeling dataset and retrain the classifier. The training pipeline does not change. It is only the label set that changes.

There are emails that require removal of forwarded markers and signatures. Or maybe the support tickets that might require removing HTML tags or template text.

So here, we simply modify **`cleaning_rules.py`**

We do not have to modify the scoring, reporting, or monitoring at all.

Similarly, if the new dataset represents legal documents, so here the prompt template will change accordingly.

So here, the old template '***write a short summary of the email chunk***' need to be changed with the new template '***Extract key obligations and deadlines from this contract section***'

Here, the prompt file changes, but the prompt version tracking logic does not.

The concept of private AI projects may often tend to fail. And, it is not because the models are weak, but because the pipelines are rigid. If changing datasets requires rewriting orchestration, logging, or monitoring, then the system is brittle.

By enforcing:

- Canonical schema
- Stable scoring outputs
- Stable logging contracts
- Stable monitoring tables

We can surely and easily create a reusable AI backbone. The dataset adaptation becomes a configuration and parser problem, not a redesign problem.

With this, we demonstrated how to adapt to a new dataset by modifying only the normalization job and labels while preserving the core architecture. This separation ensures that our private AI system is not tied to a single sample dataset but can evolve to handle new domains without structural redesign.

Summary

In this chapter we transformed our private mailroom assistant from a collection of scripts into a packaged, repeatable workflow. We created a unified configuration file and a pipeline driver that wrapped ingestion, training, scoring, summarization, optional LLM acceleration, and reporting behind a single command. We established a clear run-date convention so outputs were namespaced and never overwritten, and we introduced lightweight scheduling patterns using daily or weekly execution. Each scheduled run generated a manifest file that documented inputs, outputs, model versions, and execution timestamps, preserving traceability even in automated mode.

Later, we embedded optimized monitoring directly into the pipeline by logging job duration, error counts, and output sizes for each run. Finally, we examined how to adapt the system to new datasets by separating stable architectural components such as schema contracts, logging structure, scoring outputs, and monitoring logic from dataset-specific modules like parsers, labels, cleaning rules, and prompt templates. This separation ensured that reusability extended beyond the sample dataset and that adaptation required configuration and normalization changes rather than architectural redesign.

Index

Epilogue

I think private AI will keep growing because people will keep demanding clearer boundaries around data, computation, and accountability. In the next few years on months maybe, more organizations will see data movement as a governance issue instead of a technical detail. This change will affect how AI systems are built. While teams will still want intelligence in their workflows, they'll increasingly want it in forms that can be explained, repeated, and controlled. A private system can still be powerful, but it'll be judged by how it operates. That means looking at where assets are located, how outputs can be reproduced, and how drift is detected. The fact is, adoption won't happen because of slogans. It'll happen because a private pipeline reduces risk while still delivering useful outcomes, particularly in domains where content is sensitive and compliance demands evidence rather than intention.

That's where Spark comes in. It'll fit the profile of the problem. When we talk about private AI, we're not just talking about inference. It is basically ingestion, normalization, batching, schema discipline, run tracking, and reporting. All these steps are key to making sure the outputs are reliable. The Spark is great at taking large, disorganized data and turning it into neat, consistent sets of information. This means it's already tackling the "system" part of the AI challenge. As more teams adopt private AI, they'll need a backbone that handles routine runs, produces tables that can be queried, and supports both classic ML and optional model serving integrations. And Spark is doing all of it.

I think the future is going to be all about private AI becoming more of a regular thing, with Spark keeping everything running smoothly.

-- Ryein Twardo

Thank You

www.ingramcontent.com/pod-product-compliance
Lightning Source LLC
Chambersburg PA
CBHW080215170726
48282CB00030B/1126
9789349174160